THE 20 MOST ASKED QUESTIONS IN
FRANCHISING

What you need to know before you franchise your business

with CLIVE SAWYER
and the UK's leading franchise experts

First published in 2012 by:

Live It Publishing
27 Old Gloucester Road
London, United Kingdom.
WC1N 3AX
www.liveitpublishing.com

This book is designed to provide accurate and authoritative general
information in regard to the subject matter covered. As each business
is unique in its requirements, this book is sold with the understanding
that neither the author, the contributors nor the publisher are giving
specific business, financial or legal advice. The services of a competent
professional should be sought prior to the implementation of any
expansion models for your business.

978-1-906954-46-8 (pbk)
978-1-906954-47-5 (ebk)

Dedicated to

Diane

my long suffering Personal Assistant

CONTENTS

FOREWORD

This is Clive Sawyer's second book written in a plain speaking style to provide the reader with insight into developing a business through franchising. With the collaboration of a number of experienced and knowledgeable franchise sector professionals the author has provided a valuable guide by answering twenty of the most frequently asked questions about franchise development and operation.

Clive brings to the book a wealth of experience gained from years of assisting business owners to grow and expand their business through a number of operating models including the ever popular franchising route. Business Format Franchising is a highly effective and successful business expansion strategy worldwide and has a particularly strong track record in the UK. This is largely due to the British Franchise Association overseeing and providing self regulation in the sector since 1977.

Amongst the sound expert advice and support that is available to would be franchisors, business owners need to be aware that there are many unqualified people who purport to be franchise experts. Business owners would be well advised to only seek help from franchise professionals who are accredited to the British Franchise Association, such as Clive Sawyer and the other expert contributors in this book.

This book is not intended to be a step by step guide to franchising a business or indeed to promote franchising as a suitable model for every business. Guidance and support from reputable accredited franchise professionals before embarking down the franchise development route is essential to ensure that best chance of success and to avoid costly mistakes. Despite success never being guaranteed, reading this invaluable, insightful and practical guide will set people on the right path.

Richard Holden
Head of Franchising
Lloyds Banking Group

INTRODUCTION

The authors and contributors of this book have over 100 years combined experience of the franchise industry. Whilst advising and helping businesses to develop their franchises, there are a number of questions that are repeatedly asked. This book is a collection of these frequently asked questions and what you need to know before you franchise your business.

Following on in the style of my first book "How to Franchise Your Business – The plain speaking guide for business owners", I and four of the top franchise specialists in the country, all of whom are accredited by the British Franchise Association, have answered these most frequently asked questions in a plain speaking and easy to understand manner.

Each of the twenty questions has been designed to be answered and read in isolation of the other questions. This means that there is some repetition in the various answers however this only serves to highlight some of the very crucial elements when franchising any business.

I would like to thank my fellow contributors to this book and should you wish to find out more about any of them, a profile on each person together with their contact details can be found at the end of the book under the Author Profile section.

Clive Sawyer
Managing Director
Business Options
www.businessoptions.biz

HOW DO YOU KNOW IF FRANCHISING IS THE RIGHT WAY TO GROW A BUSINESS?

By Clive Sawyer, Managing Director, Business Options

The most important point to understand is that franchising is not the only way of expanding a business. There are many other models that can be used to expand a business however in the right context, franchising can be an excellent way to expand regionally, nationally and/or internationally. In contrast, in the wrong context franchising can be absolutely the wrong way to expand a business.

> *There are many other models that can be used to expand a business*

In order to assess whether franchising is the right expansion model for a business, it is essential not only to be clear about what franchising is, but also to have a clear understanding of

3

each of the other expansion models. By considering all of the expansion models and assessing each against the objectives of the business and the resources available it is possible to select the right expansion model for the business. Therefore in answering this question it is important to start by providing a brief explanation of the five main expansion models:

- Franchising
- Licensing
- Agencies
- Distributorships
- Acquisitions

Franchising

When people talk about franchising what they are normally referring to is "Full Business Format Franchising".

The British Franchise Association (*bfa*) defines franchising as:

"... the granting of a licence by one person (the franchisor) to another (the franchisee), which entitles the franchisee to trade under the trade mark/trade name of the franchisor and to make use of an entire package, comprising all the elements necessary to establish a previously untrained person in the business and to run it with continual assistance on a predetermined basis."

4

In simple terms, the franchisor grants a franchisee the right to operate a business using the franchised company's name, branding, products and or services, systems and processes that the franchisor has successfully and profitably operated themselves.

It is important to be clear who is who, in the franchise relationship. The *franchisor* is the company that is franchising their business. The *franchisee* is the person who buys the franchise from the franchisor.

In addition to granting of rights to the franchisee, the franchisor also needs to:

- continually develop the products and services that the franchisee sells ensuring that they remain current and competitive in the marketplace.
- provide ongoing support and guidance to the franchisee.

In return the franchisee normally pays an initial upfront fee and then ongoing monthly fees for the duration that they have the franchise.

When one thinks of Full Business Format Franchising, the best example is probably McDonalds. McDonalds is the epitome of Full Business Format franchising. Wherever a person goes in the world they can be confident about what a Big Mac will taste like, how they will be served and the total McDonalds experience.

Is Franchising Right for your Business?

In order to check whether Franchising is a suitable expansion model for a business, four questions should be asked.

1. *Do you want franchisees to trade under the company name?*

   Make an objective assessment as to whether others could sell your products or services equally well under a different brand name. If the brand name does have a major impact on the success of the business then franchising may be an appropriate expansion model. However for some businesses the trade name is not important. It is important to understand that if franchisees are going to trade under the company brand name then sophisticated internal systems and processes will need to be put in place to protect the reputation of the brand from poor performing franchisee(s).

2. *Can franchisees be taught how to run their business in the exact same way as the parent company?*

   Every system, process and procedure in the business will need to be recorded in the Franchise Operations Manual in minute detail. It is important that nothing is left to individual interpretation otherwise there will be inconsistency across the franchise network. If the Franchise Operations Manual is detailed enough then it should be possible to teach any franchisee how to run their business so that it replicates the way the parent company operates.

3. *Are you committed to providing ongoing support to your franchisees?*

Ongoing support does not mean giving franchisees a phone call once a month to see how they are doing. Ongoing support is about taking a real interest in your franchisees business and helping them to be as successful as possible. Successful franchisees will benefit the franchisor both financially and during ongoing franchisee recruitment. Conversely failing franchisees take much more of the franchisor's time, affect the franchisor's ongoing fee income and makes future franchisee recruitment much harder. Nobody wants to buy a franchise where there are unhappy failing franchisees.

> *Nobody wants to buy a franchise where there are unhappy failing franchisees*

4. *Do you want to be liable for all products and services sold?*

When businesses look to expand, the issue of liability is

normally a major concern. When expanding, businesses often worry about how they will control how their products or services are sold when large numbers of franchisees are involved. One of the benefits with franchising is that the franchisee is liable for their actions and not the franchisor. The legal contract for the sale of any product or service sold by the franchisee is between the customer and the franchisee. The only time that the franchisor may be liable is when the franchisee has been told by the franchisor how to sell the product or service and the information they are given contravened any laws, or if the franchisor provides the franchisee with products that are faulty. However having said this, it doesn't matter which expansion model is adopted, if the products are faulty the business will always be liable.

These are just a few of the key considerations when deciding whether franchising is the right expansion model for a business.

Licensing:

Licensing as a form of business expansion is not as well understood as standard company expansion or franchising. This is because licensing can take many forms. The simplest way of thinking about licensing is that the licensor grants a licensee the right to sell their products or services under the licensee's company name, not the licensor's company name. A licence is just a commercial contract laying out the terms that have been agreed with a third party, and these terms can be very varied and ultimately whatever the two parties agree on.

Without wishing to confuse, it is worth stating that Full Business Format Franchising is a form of licensing, as the franchisor grants the franchisee rights to sell their products or services. However with Full Business Format Franchising there are certain terms that must be included within the franchise agreement (contract).

When considering licensing as an expansion model it is helpful to ask the following questions:

- *How much support do you want to provide licensees with?* Normally the licensor does not have to support licensees as much as they would franchisees as the licensee will already know how to run a business. The licensors role is more focused on providing technical support relating to the products or services.

- *How important is promoting the licensors company name?* As the licensee is trading under their own name the licensor's brand name will not be promoted. This can have the advantage that if a licensee does anything wrong, there is minimal risk to the licensor's brand reputation. This is where a decision needs to be made as to how important it is for others to trade under the company brand name.

- *Is speed to market important?*

Licensees are normally existing business owners, and therefore are likely to already have their own customer database that they can market the licensor's products or services to. This means that the licensor can get their products and services into the market far quicker than they would if they had to establish new company owned outlets or waited for franchisees to set-up and establish their own business. Setting up any new outlet, whether it is company owned or a franchise will inevitably take time to get established. Another major consideration when licensing is that normally licensees are granted on a non exclusive basis. This is because the licensee isn't as reliant on the income generated from selling the licensors services or products as they will still have the income from selling their own products and services. In addition, as each licensee will have their own customer base, more than one licensee can operate in the same area without directly competing with each other. Therefore a licensor can have far more licensees selling their products or services in an area than they could have franchisees or company owned outlets in the same area. If speed of expansion or number of outlets selling your products or services is important then licensing may be a suitable expansion model.

- *Do you want to be liable for the products and services sold by licensees?*

    As previously stated, liability is normally a major concern when businesses look to expand. As with franchising, licensing removes the parent company liability. With licensing, the legal contract for the sale of any product or service is between the cus-tomer and the licensee. The only times that the licensor may be liable is when the li-censee has been told by the licensor how to sell the prod-uct or service and the infor-mation they are given con-travened any laws, or if the licensor provides the licensee with products that are faulty. So if reducing liability is important then licensing as a form of expansion should be considered.

    Liability is normally a major concern when businesses look to expand

Agencies:

When most people hear the words agents or agency they often think of door to door salespeople or Travel Agents. The key elements of an agency expansion model are that the company takes on people to sell their products and services on their behalf. The door to door salesperson will try to sell products on behalf of the company they are representing. The Travel Agent sells holidays on behalf of the holiday companies. In both cases the customer is not signing with the agent but with the original company. Therefore the original company is liable for the actions of their agents.

In the case of Travel Agents most people do not worry about buying their holiday through Travel Agents as the industry is very well regulated. The systems and processes adopted by the Travel Agents are very sophisticated and make it very difficult for Travel Agents to miss sell. This however is not always the case when it comes to other agents such as the ones that sell door to door. Often in these cases it is likely that the agent is on a commission for every sale they make. There are reported cases of door to door sales agents staying in a house for many hours trying to convince the customer to buy. This, not surprisingly, can lead to instances of miss selling.

When considering whether to adopt an agency model for expanding your business, there are some key considerations:

- *Is speed to market important?*
  There are established lists of people who are pre-pared to act as agents on behalf of a company. Therefore it can be rela-

It can be relatively quick to establish a network of agents covering the whole country

tively quick to establish a network of agents covering the whole country. In this respect agency models allow quicker expansion than company owned expansion or franchising. The agency model can also be quicker than licensing however given the right model, licensing can be just as quick in establishing national coverage.

- *Do you want to be liable for the products and services sold?*

  The liability issue is the biggest concern that people have when considering expanding using an agency model. It is important to consider whether systems and processes can be established which make it very difficult for miss selling to take place. If systems and processes can be established then agents can be a quick route to market however if it isn't possible to control how the agents sell then be cautious. Having a network of commission based agents selling remotely on your behalf may give rise to liability issues.

- *Do you want to avoid employing large numbers of staff?*

  Employing large numbers of staff and all that entails is often the reason businesses look for other expansion models rather than company expansion. On the face of it using agents rather than staff may seem a good way to avoid the staff issues. On one level that is correct, agents are not employees and therefore do not have the same rights as an employee has, however under UK and European law, self-employed agents are legally protected through indemnity agreements and compensation legislation. If a company unfairly cancels an agent's contract then they will have to pay the agent an amount reflecting the value of the work the agent has done in building up sales including the agent's efforts to identify customers and build relationships with them. With a compensation agreement, the company will have to pay the agent an amount reflecting the value of what the agent has done, and the agent's loss of future earnings. Therefore once agents have been taken on, it is not possible to terminate their contract unfairly without paying some form of compensation for their loss of earnings unless the agent was guilty of gross misconduct. In addition if the agent is self-employed, the company is liable to pay an indemnity or compensation if the agent dies or retires. It is therefore important to understand that by adopting an agency model, there will be indemnity and compensation liabilities.

Distributorships:

Expansion using distributors is mainly for businesses that have products. A distributor is a customer of yours that you sell your products to and who then has the responsibility for trying to sell them on. This has the advantage that once sold to the distributor there is no further involvement or liability for the product.

The key considerations for adopting a distributorship model are:

- *Is your brand important to you?*
  This is where there is a need to differentiate between the company trading name and the brand name of the products. Distributors sell products under their own company name and therefore the name of the company selling to the distributor will have limited visibility to the distributor's customers. Typically the company brand will only be seen on the product packaging. If awareness and promotion of a company brand is not important then distributorship, as an expansion model may be suitable.

- *Is speed to market important?*
  Using a distributor model is probably the quickest way to get products sold nationwide. There are no issues relating to commercial premises or staff as the distributor buys from the company direct and then how they want to sell them it is up to them. Distributors normally do not have exclusive territories and therefore the parent company can sell their products to any distributor who wants to buy them.

- *Is the way your products are displayed and marketed important?*
  As the distributor buys the products and is then responsible for selling them to their customers the parent company has

little or no control over how the products are sold or how they are displayed. If it is not important how the products are displayed, marketed and sold, then a distributorship model may be appropriate.

- *Do you want to be liable for the products and services sold?*
  As products are sold to the distributor the responsibility and liability theoretically ends with the distributors. If products are faulty then there may be liability issues but any liability for product miss selling lies with the distributor.

Acquisitions:

Although not normally uppermost in most people's minds when considering expansion models for a business, acquisitions should not be overlooked. Buying an established business and rebranding it can be a quick way of establishing and growing your brand. What may be surprising is that it can be relatively easy to borrow the money to buy an established business, so long as it is not overpriced. Banks will lend against the trading history and profitability of the business being bought. When

> *Buying an established business and rebranding it can be a quick way of establishing and growing your brand*

16

purchasing an existing business it is normal that one buys the assets of the business. This means that one normally buys the fixtures and fittings which can be an advantage. It is important to know however that under the Transfer of Undertakings (Protection of Employment) Regulations (TUPE) it is very likely that the purchasing company will be required to take on all the staff from the old business. This means that other than changing the name above the door a company could be ready to open virtually immediately the purchase is completed. The downside is that the staff that the company will be required to take may not be happy with the change of management or the many changes the new company might wish to implement. In addition not all the customers of the old company may want to do business with the new company.

When deciding whether expansion through acquisitions is the right model for a business the key considerations should be:

- *Are there any suitable companies that you could buy?*
  If your business operates in a marketplace with lots of competitors throughout the country then it is likely than some of these companies may be open to an acquisition; however it is important to look to buy companies that are in the right location geographically and which can work with your existing business. A company should not be tempted to purchase a business just because it finds someone who is willing to sell.

- *Do you want to take over staff from another company?*
  Given the Transfer of Undertakings (Protection of Employment) Regulations (TUPE) it is highly likely that there will be a requirement to take on the staff from the company being sold. This may inhibit who works in the company. The company may inherit some really good staff however they could equally be stuck with employees that who are not so good. When considering an acquisition one should not just think about the financial figures as the staff issues may be equally important.

Deciding which model is right for you:

Every business is different and every business owner has different influencing factors. Therefore there is no definitive answer to which expansion model is right for a specific business.

The decision as to which expansion model to adopt may be the most important decision a business takes, therefore it is important that the decision is not rushed. Whichever model is chosen the company must be totally committed to it, otherwise they risk wasting a lot of money and effort. A wrong decision could damage the business, possibly irrevocably.

This may sound like a recommendation not to ever expand a business; nothing could be further from the truth. Done correctly expanding a business can be financially and morally fulfilling and the opportunity for a business owner to grow from a single outlet into a regional, national, and or international brand can be very exciting. It can provide business owners with

Take time to objectively consider all the various options for expansion

far greater wealth and open opportunities that can not be achieved by staying a small company. So it is essential to take time to objectively consider all the various options for expansion and when a decision is taken, to commit to it with total conviction.

It may be that some readers will never get past this first chapter, having decided that franchising is not right for them. If that is the case then the small price of this book may have saved you a fortune, and I wish you every success with your business. For those of you that either want to find out more about franchising or have decided that franchising is right for them, read on.

CAN A BUSINESS OWNER FRANCHISE THEIR BUSINESS THEMSELVES OR DO THEY HAVE TO USE PROFESSIONAL FRANCHISE ADVISERS?

By Clive Sawyer, Managing Director, Business Options

In the UK there are no specific franchise laws or regulations. This means that there is nothing to prevent a business owner from developing their own franchise model and all the supporting documentation and marketing their franchise without any professional advice and assistance. Even when it comes to the franchise agreement, a business owner is totally within their rights to download a template franchise agreement from the internet, tailoring it themselves and then getting a prospective

> *"Why would a business owner use professional franchise advisers rather than doing it all themselves?"*

franchisee to sign it. So the simple answer to this question is no, a business owner does not have to use professional franchise advisers. If this is the case then maybe the more appropriate question should be: "why would a business owner use professional franchise advisers rather than doing it all themselves?"

There are many things in life that we are allowed to do ourselves like plastering a wall, or changing the brake pads on a car, but how many of us would feel confident that we could do as good a job as a qualified professional. I believe that I could learn from a book or the internet the right quantities or materials to mix up plaster. I can also learn the right tools to use and even the technique to use, but this doesn't mean that I will end up with a glass smooth finish to my wall if a plaster it myself. I am sure if I tried to plaster a wall the end result would be adequate, so the question is whether adequate is good enough? To do most jobs really well requires training and experience. Some of it comes from knowing the tricks of the trade; other elements will be knowing what works and what doesn't.

This also applies when it comes to franchising a business. A business owner can read books on the subject and attend franchise seminars which will give them a basic understanding of what is involved in franchising a business. I often tell business owners that eighty percent of franchising a business is common business acumen. It is the other twenty percent which are the tricks of the trade and the knowledge of what works and more importantly what doesn't work. It then comes down to how well the business owner wants to franchise their business. If they are happy with an adequate franchise model and supporting material then there is compelling argument for a business owner to save money and franchise their business themselves without the help and assistance of professional franchise advisers. If however the business owner wants the best chance for success, they would be well advised to take advantage of the knowledge and experience of professional franchise advisers.

There are many elements to successfully franchising a business and each of these requires specific skills, knowledge and expertise. It is important to use professional advisers who are accredited in each specific area of the business. It is very unlikely that any one professional adviser will have skills in all areas and therefore a business owner will need to create a team of professional franchise advisers. This is no different from running any business, since one would not expect a business owner to be highly experienced in every aspect of their business. It is very rare to find a business owner who is an expert in all their products and services they sell as well as being an expert in all the legal aspects of their business, all human resource issues and employment law, product development, IT, marketing and sales. Successful businesses bring in people with the expertise and experience in each area of their business to maximise its potential. This should be the same approach to use when franchising.

The Franchise Development Model

The first step when franchising a business should always be the franchise development model. This assesses both the viability of franchising as well as creating the detailed blueprint that all other steps in the franchising process will refer to. Franchising in this respect is no different from any other project a business may undertake. The first step must be to develop a detailed plan that all other aspects of implementing the plan can continually refer back to.

Business planning is a skill that many business owners will already possess and may have put into practice many times. When it comes to the franchise development plan, most business owners will probably have the ability to do eighty percent of it, however it is the remaining twenty percent which is specific to franchising that the business owner is unlikely to have the skills, experience or knowledge to do properly

Without a robust plan all the other elements of the implementation will be ineffectual

themselves. This planning stage is the most important element to get right. Without a robust plan all the other elements of the implementation will be ineffectual as they will be implementing a flawed plan. A business owner can read all the franchise books available and attend numerous franchise seminars however, it is unlikely they will be able to develop as good and robust a franchise development plan as an accredited professional franchise adviser. Setting the correct upfront price and ongoing fee structure is not just a scientific calculation. Correct pricing requires a knowledge of the whole franchise industry, what other franchises charge and not just those direct franchise competitors but any franchise that is targeting the same profile of prospective franchisee. Correct pricing also relies on an in-depth understanding of the expected return on investment that franchisees look for, as well as an understanding of what level of ongoing fees will be perceived as acceptable depending on the services the franchisor will provide their franchisees. How the franchisor will take their fees is another consideration, should it be as a percentage of the franchisees turnover, a fixed monthly fee, a mark-up on products supplied to the franchisee, or a combination of two or more of these? Setting the right upfront and ongoing fee structure requires skills, knowledge and experience.

The franchise model does not just concern itself with the franchisee fees, it also covers all other aspects of the franchise, from the size and make of a franchisees territory, to the length of time the franchise will be granted for. The franchise model also looks at the services the franchisor will provide, what legal structure the franchisee should operate under, whether they need to be VAT registered, and what the process is for a franchisee who wants to sell their franchise. Other areas covered in the franchise model will be: whether there will be minimum performance levels that the franchisee must meet and what happens if they fail to achieve these; when the franchisee has to pay their ongoing fees; whether any regional variance will be permitted within the franchise network; who will handle national or key account customers; what internal systems and processes franchisees must use and whether these use centralised accounting software, client management databases, invoicing issuing and collection systems.

The franchise development model must address all the above areas and create a franchise business model that works for both the franchisor and its franchisees. Get this right and the business stands every chance of having a successful franchise, but get it wrong, even if it doesn't fail, it will fail to realise the true potential of the business. Using an experienced accredited franchise consultant to help develop the franchise development model will ensure that all aspects of the franchise have been covered and the final model will be right for the business.

The Franchise Agreement

Once the franchise model has been successfully developed the first step in its implementation should be the legal documents. It is important to check at this early stage that the model does not break any laws. There are few things worse than creating all the systems and process for a franchise as well as the franchisee recruitment strategy and supporting recruitment documentation only to find the model needs to be changed because it breaks a law. Often these laws will be things that a business owner may not have come across in the normal course of business such as: Vertical block exemption, the trading schemes act and price fixing rules.

Most people accept that they need to use a lawyer when dealing with legal issues. However choosing the right lawyer for the particular legal issue is just as important. Most people would not dream of using a divorce lawyer to deal with a commercial property issue, or an intellectual property lawyer to create customer terms and conditions.

To ensure than the franchise legal documents are right for the business it is essential to use an accredited franchise lawyer

Therefore when a business needs the legal documents for its franchise it should use a specialist franchise lawyer and not a general commercial lawyer. Typically a franchise lawyer accredited by the British Franchise Association will be more expensive than a general commercial lawyer however, it is critical that the franchise legal documents provide proper protection for both the franchisor and its franchisees. To ensure than the franchise legal documents are right for the business it is essential to use an accredited franchise lawyer. Cost is almost always an issue when franchising a business, however the cost to a business of not having proper franchise legal documents that have been tailored to the business can be far more in the long term than the slightly higher fees of using an accredited franchise lawyer to create them at the start.

Franchise Operations Manuals

The Franchise Operations Manual is the document(s) that tells franchisees exactly how to operate their franchised business. The Franchise Operations Manual should be extremely detailed leaving nothing to misinterpretation. Misinterpretation of an Operations Manual can lead to a network of franchisees operating in slightly different ways. This in turn, will lead to issues which could potentially damage the brand and may affect the value of the business for both the franchisor and the franchisees within its network. So what role does a professional franchiser adviser play when it comes to the Franchise Operations Manual?

I believe that it is just as bad for a business owner to get a professional franchise adviser to write their Franchise

Operations Manual totally for them as it is for a business owner to write their own Franchise Operations Manual with no assistance from a professional franchise adviser. Clearly a business owner will know how their business operates and therefore they should be in the best position to document all the processes. Given that franchising is based upon the concept of replication it is essential that the Franchise Operations Manual accurately documents how the business currently operates and does not include new ways that have not been tested. A professional franchise adviser will never have the detailed knowledge about the business as the owner and therefore there is a real risk of elements being missed out if a professional franchise adviser writes the Franchise Operations Manual in isolation.

I do however believe that the professional franchise adviser does have a role in supporting the business owner in creating the Franchise Operation Manual. The professional franchise adviser can provide input as to the various franchise specific sections that need to be included in a Franchise Operations Manual, which are different to the technical sections on how to market and sell the products and/or services of the business. The professional franchise adviser can also explain the most appropriate format and layout of a Franchise Operations manual and how it should be used and updated. They can play an invaluable role in reviewing the Franchise Operations Manual to ensure that it is clear, unambiguous and can be understood by someone with no or limited industry experience, which is likely to be the position of the franchise.

Recruiting Franchisees

The key to the success of any franchise is being able to recruit appropriate and suitable franchisees. A business can develop a first rate franchise model and all the supporting documents however this is no good if they fail to recruit suitable franchisees. Given that the whole success of the franchise relies on this, will a business owner have the experience and knowledge of where and how to best market their franchise opportunity? There are dozens of different franchise websites that a business can advertise their franchise on and four or five dedicated franchise magazines. Then there are regional and national franchise exhibitions, and the franchise sections of national newspapers and that's before one starts to consider other less mainstream franchise publications such as those targeted at the armed forces.

> *The key to the success of any franchise is being able to recruit appropriate and suitable franchisees*

Most business owners do not have a bottomless franchisee recruitment budget and therefore it is important that they spend their budget in the most appropriate and cost effective way. A professional franchise adviser will have the knowledge, based on the franchisee profile developed in the franchise development model, of which are the most appropriate franchise marketing media to use and just as critically when during the year to use each. It may be that advertising in a franchise magazine is deemed a good way for the business to advertise its franchise, however without industry knowledge a business owner may not realise that advertising in a certain publication during the month of one of the national franchise exhibitions has the added benefit that the magazine is given away free to over 4,000 people who attend the exhibition. A business owner may also not be aware of the franchise features lists that the national newspapers have. These list the sector that the paper will focus on in the franchise section each week during the year, whereas a professional franchise adviser will.

A professional franchiser adviser will also be able to advise on other non franchise media that may be appropriate to market the franchise opportunity. They will also be able to advise on the other non advertising types of marketing that may be appropriate such as PR, direct mail, and social media. Given the importance of getting the franchise recruitment marketing right, using a professional franchise adviser can repay the upfront cost of the adviser many times over through the business being able to maximise the use of the franchisee recruitment budget.

Knowing which adviser to use

Hopefully I have been able to demonstrate why a business owner should employ the services of professional franchise advisers when franchising their business, however how do they know which adviser to use?

One of the biggest problems with the franchise industry being unregulated is that any person can advertise their services as a professional franchise adviser. A simple search on the internet will bring up a number of companies stating that they can franchise your business for a low fixed fee. These companies seem to say everything that a business owner wants to hear and all at a very cheap price, but then that is where alarm bells should start to ring. Why can they do it so much cheaper than others? Remember these people pertaining to be professional franchise advisers are not going to tell you that they aren't very good. A number of them are very good sales people and are well practiced at knowing just what to say to a business owner. Unfortunately there are hundreds of astute business owners that have been caught out and have wasted both their time and money on failed franchise ventures, many of which never get off the ground.

The only body that accredits franchise advisers in the UK is the British Franchise Association (bfa). All franchise advisers accredited by the bfa have gone through a rigorous accreditation process and therefore a business owner has the comfort in knowing that they don't have to just rely on what they are being told by a franchise adviser but that this is backed up by the bfa's accreditation process. Therefore if a business owner is looking to use a professional franchise adviser, their first place to look should be the bfa's website at www.thebfa.org. If any franchise adviser tells a business owner that they chose

All franchise advisers accredited by the bfa have gone through a rigorous accreditation process

not to become bfa accredited then the business owner should ask themselves "why would any professional franchise adviser not want to be accredited by the only franchise association in the UK"? The real reason is most likely to be because they wouldn't pass the bfa's accreditation process. If a business owner accepts the value a professional franchise adviser can bring when franchising a business, they need to make sure the adviser is an accredited franchise adviser and not just someone masquerading as a franchise adviser.

WHAT ARE THE KEY STEPS WHEN FRANCHISING A BUSINESS AND HOW LONG DOES IT TAKE?

By Clive Sawyer, Managing Director, Business Options

What are the key steps when franchising a business and how long does it take?

The keys steps when franchising a business are very similar to the steps taken when developing and implementing any project. In its simplest terms the first step is develop the project model, create any legal documentation required by the model, then put the internal systems and processes in place to run and manage the project once launched. Finally one develops a strategy and the supporting marketing material to tell customers about the products or services being sold. Franchising a business follows the same process with the addition of some elements specific to franchising. The table overleaf is a summary of the phases involved in franchising a business. The first three phases are concerned with the development and launch of a franchise, with phase 4 and 5 being concerned with supporting a franchise network and selling the business from both a franchisee and franchisor perspective.

The Franchise Development Process includes 5 major phases

The Franchise Development Process

Phase One Franchise Development Model	Phase Two Infrastructure Development	Phase Three Franchisee Recruitment	Phase Four Franchise Support	Phase Five Franchise Exit Planning
Assesses the viability of franchising a business and creates the Franchise Model which will be the blueprint that all other phases of the franchise development refers to. • Franchise Development Model	Creates all the systems, processes and support material required to run and manage a franchise network. • Systems and Process Development • Legal Documents • Trade Marking • Operations Manual • Territory Mapping • Training Programme Development	Creates the strategy for recruiting franchisees, as well as the process and material required to handling enquiries. • Franchise Recruitment Strategy • Recruitment Material • Sales Enquiry Processing • Franchisee Interviewing • Recruitment Processing • Franchisee Business Plan • Franchisee Training	Identifies the support a franchisor will need to help them run and manage their network of franchisees. • Franchisor Support • Franchise Support Staff Recruitment • Franchise Support Staff Training • Network Meetings and Conferences	Provides the technical support and advice on how to sell the franchise business for both the franchisor and franchisees. • Franchisor & Franchisee Exit Planning • Franchisor Sales • Franchisee Re-Sales

Phase 1: Franchise Development Model

The Franchise Development Model is the most crucial step in the whole franchise development process. This is because without having a clear detailed plan of how the franchise needs to be structured to make it successful for both the franchisor and franchisees, there is virtually no chance of success. If the plan is right at the outset then everything else will fall into place.

The Franchise Development Model is the most crucial step in the whole franchise development process

The Franchise Development Model will be the document from which all the franchise legal documentation will be based upon. Having a clear understanding of roles and responsibilities for both franchisor and franchisee, as stated in the Franchise Development Model will form the structure for the Franchise Operations Manual. The Franchise Recruitment Strategy and supporting Franchise Recruitment Material will be dependent on having a clear profile of the type of person who would be suited as a franchisee and what their key drivers will be when deciding whether the franchise is right for them. Developing a franchisee profile and the key decision drivers for franchisees is an integral part of the Franchise Development Model. In short, the most important element of any franchise is the Franchise Development Model.

What should be included in a Franchise Development Model?

Without wishing to over simplify the question, it should include everything. However, there are a number of core elements that any Franchise Development Model should include, these being:

- The Franchise Package
- The Terms of the Franchise
- The Role of the Franchisee and the Franchisor
- The Financial Projections for both the Franchisee and Franchisor
- The Obligations for both the Franchisee and Franchisor

The Franchise Package

The Franchise Package includes the Initial Franchise Fee, the Franchise Set-Up Package, the Franchisee Working Capital requirement, and any additional capital costs for the franchisee. This should show prospective franchisees what the total investment required is and the payment terms.

The Terms of the Franchise

The terms of the franchise are those elements that dictate how the franchise is structured such as: the number of years the franchise will be granted for, the ongoing fee structure, the legal entity the franchisee must adopt, terms relating to VAT and

Data Protection registration, sale and renewal of the franchise, the premises that franchisees can operate from, the criteria for territories, the policy regarding national accounts, ongoing training of the franchisee and any staff they may have, and what happens if the franchisee is incapacitated or worse dies.

The Role of the Franchisee and the Franchisor

When developing a franchise model it is critical to identify the roles and responsibilities for both the franchisor and franchisees. The franchisor needs to be clear about what their franchisees will be responsible for and what they will provide for them. One of the biggest mistakes that business owners make when developing their franchise is to expect the franchisee to do everything. Most franchisees do not have extensive business experience. This means that they will not have the skills and experience to competently undertake every aspect of their franchise.

The type of person suited as a franchisee depends on what they will need to do in their franchise

Having worked out the roles and responsibilities for the franchisee and franchisor it is important to identify what type of person would be suited to be a franchisee. This is called the franchisee profile. The type of person suited as a franchisee depends on what they will need to do in their franchise.

The Financial Projections for both the Franchisee and Franchisor

The success of all franchisees is intrinsically linked to the financial profitability of both the franchisor and their franchisees. Too often all the emphasis is on the projected franchisee profitability with scant regard with the profitability of the franchisor.

The franchisee:

When creating franchisee projections it is essential that these are done conservatively. This should not be an exercise in target inflated sales projections otherwise all that will happen is that the franchisees will underachieve leading to a demotivated franchisee network. When developing franchisee financial projections it is critical to produce detailed monthly and annual Profit and Loss, Cash Flow and Product Sales projections. Even though franchisees are provided with these financial projections it is important to ensure they are advised to tailor them to fit their own circumstances.

Franchisor Projections:

I have had business owners question why we need to create franchisor projections believing that they only need to create franchisee projections as they are only selling to franchisees.

Often in an attempt to make the franchise package as attractive as possible to help the process of selling franchises, a franchisor forgets the impact on their own business. The long term future of the whole franchise, including that of the franchisees within the network relies on the franchisor being successful. Therefore every business owner considering franchising should create detailed monthly and annul Profit & Loss and Cash Flow projections based on both conservative levels of franchisee recruitment and conservative franchisee performance.

The Obligations for both the Franchisee and Franchisor

Many of the obligations on the franchisee may seem obvious, however to avoid any confusion and difficulties in the future it is far better to state them at the outset. Typically franchisee obligations would include:

- To pay the franchisor in an accurate and timely manner
- To operate in strict accordance with the Operations Manner
- To uphold the confidentiality of all aspects of the franchisors and franchisees business
- To ensure that all staff are trained to the level required to competently operate within the business
- Not to do anything that will bring the franchisor or the franchisor's brand into disrepute

- To take all reasonable steps to realise the potential of their business in their territory
- To attend all franchisee meetings and training

As a franchise needs to successfully work for both franchisees and the franchisor, there needs to be obligations on the franchisor. Typically franchisor obligations would include:

- Training the franchisee to a competent level to successfully run their franchised business.
- To help the franchisee set-up and launch their business
- To provide ongoing support and advice in a timely manner
- To research and develop products and services for their franchisee network to ensure that their businesses remain competitive in their marketplace.
- To take all reasonable steps to protect the franchisee's business
- To protect the franchisors brand and reputation
- To take quick and incisive action to stop any unsuitable action by franchisees within their network

The Franchise Development Model – Summary:

Some business owners may question whether all this planning is really necessary and can't they just get going with franchising their business. However, if they get the Franchise Development Model right it will be the blueprint that all other areas of the franchise development will refer to, and it will give them their best chance for success. Having created a robust Franchise Development Model, all that remains to do is to implement it.

Phase 2: Infrastructure Development

Infrastructure development is about making sure that all the systems and processes are suitable for a network of nationwide franchisees. These systems and processes are usually split into two categories: 1) Head Office Systems 2) Franchise Operating Systems.

1. *Head Office Systems*

   These are the systems and processes that will be required to enable the business owner to carry out their role as the franchisor. They will need to review whether the systems and processes that they currently use are appropriate for use with a network of franchisees spread across the country.

2. *Franchise Operating Systems*

   Before any franchisees are recruited, the franchisor must review all the systems and processes that their franchisees will follow whilst carrying out their day to day business, and assess whether they are all in place and fit for purpose.

Legal Requirements

As franchising is a legal contract between the franchisor and the franchisee, there needs to be a legal document setting out the conditions under which the franchisee is buying the franchise, the obligations on both franchisor and franchisee and what happens if any of these conditions or obligations are broken. It is for this reason that franchisees are required to sign a "Franchise Agreement". However depending on the way the franchise is structured, there will be a number of other legal documents that are also required. The main legal documents that are used in franchising are:

- Confidentiality Agreement
- Deposit Agreement
- Franchise Agreement
- Commercial Lease Agreement
- Software License Agreement
- Intellectual Property Assignment Rights
- Employment Contracts
- Telephone Transfer Agreement

There is also one other key legal process that all franchisors needs to consider, Trade Marking. If a franchisee is going to trade under the brand of the franchisor then it is important that the brand name is protected to stop other companies trading under the same or similar names in other parts of the country. The only way to protect against another business operating under the same or similar name is to Trade Mark it. This is a relatively straight forward process and can either be done online through the Intellectual Property Office or through many solicitors and Trade Mark Registration companies. For further information about Trade Marking, visit the Intellectual Property Office at www.ipo.gov.

> *The only way to protect against another business operating under the same or similar name is to Trade Mark it*

Franchise Operations Manual

The Franchise Operations Manual is one of the most critical parts of any franchise. The Franchise Operations Manual provides all the detailed instructions on how a franchisee must operate their business and forms, along with the Franchise Agreement, the legal conditions under which the franchisee will operate.

43

A common question I get asked is how much detail does one need to go into when creating a Franchise Operations Manual. The answer is very straight forward; it is as detailed as it needs to be to ensure that every franchisee operates exactly the same way. Unfortunately most Franchise Operations Manuals have far too little detail. When a company's brand is at the mercy of their franchisees, they should take every reasonable action to minimize the risk of one or more of their franchisees doing something, which ultimate damages the reputation of the business.

The only way to ensure that every franchisee operates in exactly the same way is to leave nothing to misinterpretation

The only way to ensure that every franchisee operates in exactly the same way is to leave nothing to misinterpretation. The Franchise Operations Manual has to state, in minute detail, everything a franchisee should do and how they should do it.

As a Franchise Operations Manual covers every part of the franchisees business, and given that every business is slightly different, there is no such thing as a template Franchise Operations Manual. The only real use for a template Franchise Operations Manual is to provide an idea of some of the topics that you may need to be included. However, having said that every Franchise Operations Manual is different there two distinct elements to the Manual: 1) Setting up and running a franchised business 2) selling and delivering the products and services of the company.

Franchise Training Programme

Once a person signs the Franchise Agreement they become a franchisee. However, before they can be permitted to start trading they must be trained in all aspects of the franchise business. When it comes to franchisee training it is not sufficient for a franchisee just to "turn up" for their training, it is important that when completed, they are trained to a standard suitable to start operating the franchise. Most franchisors will include some form of testing and accreditation within the franchise training model and should a franchisee fail to achieve the necessary standard, then the franchisor can insist the franchisee attend additional training at their own cost to bring them up to the required standard, or the franchise may be revoked.

When developing a franchisee training programme a good starting point is the Franchise Operations Manual. As a Franchise Operations Manual should detail everything needed for a franchisee to run their business, it would make sense to use the Franchise Operations Manual as the base for the franchisee training. In some franchise training courses, the franchisor will start on page 1 of the Franchise Operations Manual and go through every page until they get to the end. Other franchisors use the Franchise Operations Manual as a reference document and divide the franchisee training into two distinct parts 1) How to run a franchised business 2) how to sell and deliver the products and services of the franchise.

Clearly the information contained in this section of the Franchisee Training course will differ for each franchise. The training can be done in a classroom format or offsite and undertaken in a real situation through working with someone already doing the role. Whichever approach is taken it is still good practice to keep referring back to the Franchise Operations Manual on the basis that the manual should contain everything the franchisee needs.

The duration of the franchisee training will also vary between franchises. The franchise training programme should be as long as is necessary to cover every aspect of the franchised business and to ensure that franchisees are competent to start trading.

Franchise Business Plan

The franchise business plan is an essential tool for the franchisee both for raising any funding needed to purchase and operate the franchise, as well as a tool to monitor a franchisees progress and keep the business focused on achieving its goals.

Many franchisees will not have created a complete Business Plan before, which is why it is common practice for franchisors to provide a Business Plan template. It is important however to stress that franchisees must personalise any Business Plan template to reflect the specific conditions in their franchise territory.

The Franchise Business Plan must meet the needs of the individual franchisee. The franchisee needs, amongst other things, to be clear about the potential in their territory, what the competition is and the pricing structure required for them to be successful in their territory. Only by understanding the market that they are going to be operating in and the local influencing factors can they stand any chance of running a successful franchised business. Although franchising is about every franchise operating in exactly the same way, there will be different influencing factors on franchisees depending on where they are located, the market potential in their area and who their competitors will be. A successful franchisee is one who understands the market they are operating in and discusses any local factors that may have an influence on their business with their franchisor.

> *A successful franchisee is one who understands the market they are operating in*

Franchise Territory Mapping

The majority of franchises operate on an exclusive territory basis. This means that every franchisee will be given a map showing an area where they will be the only franchisee in the franchise network who will be allowed to market their business in.

When a franchise model is based on exclusive territories it is important to ensure that the criteria used to define the territories are based upon the key influencing factors for the business. The most common influencing factor is having sufficient potential customers in an area necessary to generate the level of business required for a franchisee to be successful.

Phase 3: Franchise Recruitment

The final steps in franchising a business relates to franchisee recruitment. Franchise recruitment can be split into four main areas: 1) Recruitment strategy, 2) Recruitment Material, 3) Recruitment processing, 4) Training and set-up.

1. **Recruitment Strategy:**
    Much of the success in any franchise is down to having the right people as franchisees. If a business has the right people as their franchisees who have both the skills and correct mental attitude required then there is every chance that with the right training and ongoing support they will

be successful. Conversely recruit the wrong people and it will create far more work for the franchisor, will hamper future franchisee recruitment and will ultimate make less money for both the franchisor and the franchisee.

> *The success in any franchise is down to having the right people as franchisees*

They golden rule in franchisee recruitment is to develop a profile of the type of people most suited to being a franchisee of the business and only recruiting those that meet this profile exactly.

Having drawn up the ideal franchise profile, something that should be done in the initial Franchise Development Model, it is then possible to develop a marketing strategy that is directed at the right type of people and in the right media.

Recruitment Strategy Objectives:
It would be easy to think that the franchisee recruitment strategy was purely about marketing the franchise opportunity in a place where potential franchisees might see it. However the franchise recruitment strategy objectives are more complex that just that. The recruitment strategy has four key objectives:

1. Generate an awareness of the franchise opportunity
2. Build confidence in the brand
3. Provide comprehensive information to prospective franchisees
4. Operate a recruitment process that identifies suitable franchisees

By ensuring the right people know about the franchise, using appropriate types of media, conveying the right message about the business will enable the franchisor to generate the right type of enquiries about their franchise.

Once the franchise profile has been created, the franchisor needs to decide where and how to market.

I have specifically talked about marketing the franchise opportunity rather than advertising the franchise opportunity as advertising is only one type of marketing. Marketing is a highly complex topic and there have been thousands of books written on the subject. The Chartered Institute of marketing defines marketing as "The management process responsible for identifying, anticipating and satisfying customer requirements profitably." There are many different processes that can be used for letting prospective franchisees know that you are offering a franchise. Five of the main ways used to market a franchise are:

- Online
- Off the page
- Exhibitions, Shows & Events
- Press Releases
- Word of Mouth

There are of course many other ways that can be used to market a franchise opportunity such as: direct mail campaigns, in store posters and shop windows advertisements, in street signage such as bill boards and telephone kiosks, train station signs, specific sector media such as armed forces media, ethnic minority media, gay media, and media targeting the over 50's.

Franchise Recruitment Plan:
When developing any strategy, whether it is how to recruit franchisees or how to launch a new product or service, it is important to formalise it by writing it down. Having created a clear franchisee profile and identified the various media that your franchisee profile person sees and hears, it is essential to create a franchise recruitment plan.

The franchise recruitment plan is a twelve month plan showing what media will be used and when to market

Use a mix of different marketing media

your franchise opportunity. When creating your marketing plan it is often a good idea to use a mix of different marketing media.

2. **Franchise Recruitment Material:**
   Having developed the franchise recruitment strategy the next step is to create all the forms, documents and letters required to process enquiries for the franchise. These forms, documents and letters are then combined together to form your franchise recruitment pack.

   The franchise recruitment pack should contain everything required to handle an initial enquiry right through to signing up a franchise. Typically a franchise recruitment pack will contain fifteen to twenty different pieces of recruitment material and can include amongst others:

   1. Franchise Recruitment Process Map
   2. Franchise Enquiry Form
   3. Franchise Brochure
   4. Franchise Brochure Letter
   5. Franchise Application Form
   6. Franchise Application Form Letter
   7. Invitation to a Franchise Interview Letter
   8. Decline for a Franchise Interview Letter
   9. Confirmation of a Franchise Interview Letter
   10. Confidentiality Agreement

11. Franchise Disclosure Pack
12. Provisional Franchise Offer Letter
13. Franchise Rejection Letter
14. Deposit Agreement
15. Deposit Agreement Letter
16. Franchise Agreement
17. Franchise Agreement Letter
18. Reference Request Letter
19. Formal Franchise Offer Letter
20. Franchise Training Confirmation Letter

3. **Enquiry Processing:**

   Initial Enquiry Handling Plan:

   As with the other steps in franchising a business, for this step to be effective a detailed franchise enquiry processing plan should be created. This will state the franchise enquiry handling objectives, identify what is going to be done at each stage of the enquiry handling process and indicate when each task will take place, and who will perform each task.

   There are a number of critical steps in the enquiry handling process, these include:

   1. Responding to initial enquiries and sending basic information about the franchise (Franchise Brochure/Prospectus)
   2. Sending a Franchise Application form to those still interested having read the Franchise Brochure

3. Franchisee interview to explain in detail about the franchise and assessing whether the individual is suitable to be a franchisee
4. Making the Franchise Provisional Offer
5. The applicant being sent and reviewing the Franchise Agreement
6. The applicant asking questions about the Franchise Agreement
7. The franchisor taking references on the applicant
8. The franchisor issuing a Formal Franchise Offer
9. Signing the Franchise Agreement and paying the balance of the franchise cost

These nine steps can be supplemented with additional steps such as meeting existing franchisees and shadowing them in action, or psychometric profiling of the applicant. These additional steps should be tailored to the specific requirements of the business and the role of the franchisee to help assess an applicant's suitability.

4. **Franchisee Training & Set-Up**

Once a person has signed the franchise agreement and paid their franchise fees, the last step in the franchise recruitment process is getting the franchisee ready to start trading. This will involve training the franchisee in all aspects of the franchise business as well getting the franchisee set-up to start trading.

Franchisee Training:

The most critical step in ensuring that a franchisee is going to be successful and operate according to the franchisor's rules is the franchisee training. The content, length and format of the franchisee training will vary for each franchise, however all franchisee training will cover three areas:

1. How to run a business
2. The technical elements of the product or service the franchisee will sell
3. Franchise specific requirements

Franchisee Set-Up:

This step is concerned with providing the franchisee with all the equipment required to operate their franchisee and helping them set up their business so that they are in a position to start trading.

How long does it take to franchise a business?

As with most things, there is no definitive answer to how long it should take to franchise a business. Factors that will influence the length of time will be: how much the owner wishes to do themselves and how much external support they will get from a franchise professional; how much spare time and resources the business owner has to dedicate to franchising; how complex their business is; whether their existing systems and process are suitable for supporting a franchise network; and whether they want or need to run a franchise pilot.

Typically, businesses that use the services of franchise professionals throughout the franchising process can usually be in a position to start marketing their franchise opportunity within 5 months from starting the Franchise Development Model. The more a business owner does themselves, the longer the process usually takes. I have known some businesses take eighteen months to franchise because they wanted to undertake much of the franchise development themselves and

Getting the plan right at the outset is critical

this had to be fitted around the day to day requirements of running their business. The saving in money gained by doing much of the franchise development oneself needs to be balanced against the increased length of time before the owner will be in a position to start recruiting franchisees and recouping their financial investment in developing the franchise.

Summary:

There are many steps in successfully franchising a business however these are very similar to the steps taken when developing and implementing any business project. Getting the plan right at the outset is critical as every other step in the process will refer back to it.

Successfully franchising a business takes time. Short cutting the process so that one can start marketing a franchise opportunity sooner may seem appealing however if the franchise model and supporting infrastructure is flawed then the saving in time achieved is a false saving and can create more long lasting damage to the business compared to the benefits of saving a couple of months in the set-up process.

HOW DO YOU SET THE PRICE OF A FRANCHISE AND THE LEVEL OF ONGOING FEES?

By Clive Sawyer, Managing Director, Business Options

Before setting the price of a franchise and the ongoing fees that will be charged, it is important to understand what each is made up of.

The Franchise Price:
This is the fee that a person pays to become a franchisee and normally covers the granting of the right to become a franchisee, the franchisee's initial training and loan of the Franchise Operations Manual.

This initial Franchisee Fee is normally relatively low and in the region of £5,000 to £20,000. When people see a franchise advertised for £200,000 it is important to understand that this isn't just the Franchise Fee but will also include the Franchise Set-Up Package and often the Working Capital required by the

> *The whole concept of franchising is that the franchisor should have a vested interest in maintaining the success of their franchisees*

franchisee. Although there are no laws restricting the level of the Franchise Fee charged, the British Franchise Association and most professionals within the Franchise Industry do not look favourably on high Franchise Fees. This is because the whole concept of franchising is that the franchisor should have a vested interest in maintaining the success of their franchisees.

Where a franchise is structured to allow the franchisor to make large sums from selling franchises, there is a real temptation that the franchisor will sell to anyone with the necessary funds regardless as to whether they are suitable. If this is the case the franchisor will likely be unconcerned about their franchisees success as they know that if the franchisee fails, they can make money by taking back the franchise and selling it to someone else. In this scenario the franchisor is in the business of selling franchisees rather than in establishing a successful franchise network.

The Franchise Fee includes only the loan of the Franchise Operations Manual. The reason that the Franchise Operations Manual is only lent to the franchisee and not given to the franchisee as part of the Franchise Fee is that at the end of the franchise it is important that the Franchise Operations Manual is returned to the franchisor as it contains all information, in minute detail relating to the franchisor's business. If the Franchise Operations Manual was given to the franchisee they would then own the Franchise Operations Manual and it would be much harder to enforce restrictions over what the franchisee does with it and who they show it to.

The Franchise Set-Up Package:
In the UK most franchises are sold as turnkey businesses. This means that a person buys a franchise and the franchisor provides them with everything they need to set-up and operate their business. This has distinct advantages to both the franchisor and the franchisee.

> *In the UK most franchises are sold as turnkey businesses*

From the franchisors perspective, this ensures that each franchise is set-up identically. The franchisor can source all the necessary equipment from suppliers that they have approved. Where commercial premises are involved, the franchisor will use approved shop fitters to fit out the premises. By adopting a turnkey approach the franchisor ensures consistency throughout their franchise network.

From the franchisees perspective, a turnkey franchise is very attractive as they do not have to spend time coordinating the set-up of the franchise business. In many instances the franchisee will have no experience of setting up a business from scratch and therefore having the franchisor do it for them will ensure a better end result which often will be quicker to achieve and cost less than if the franchisee had to do it all themselves.

The content of the Franchise Set-Up Package will vary with each franchise. For a restaurant franchise the Franchise Set-Up Package will include the design and decoration of the restaurant and the shop front. It will include the equipping of the kitchens and front of house as well as providing all the tables, chairs, crockery, glasses, tills, menus etc. In short everything the restaurant will need to start operating. In the case of a pet food delivery franchise, the Franchise Set-Up Package may include a sign written van, uniform, initial stock, a computerized customer ordering system, marketing brochures and catalogues, a sat nav etc. Again the Set-Up Package should include everything the franchisee needs to start operating their pet food delivery franchise.

One key element that I believe should be included in almost every Franchise Set-Up Packages, unless there is really good reason not to, is an initial launch marketing campaign. When any franchisee starts, it is important that the franchisee has success early on from both a financially and motivational point of view. The best way to ensure this is to have an initial launch marketing campaign, which will promote the franchisees new business is the most appropriate way. There are two different views when it comes to who should manage the initial launch marketing campaign; the franchisor or the franchisee. In most cases I believe that the franchisor is in the best place to ensure the initial launch marketing campaigns takes place in its entirety. By including the initial launch marketing campaign within the Franchise Set-Up Package, it ensures that the franchisor has the money to implement the initial launch marketing campaign and there is no delay. There are many cases where responsibility for instigating the launch marketing campaign is passed to the franchisee and it only partially happens or not at all.

Working Capital:

It is important that franchisees have sufficient Working Capital to let them operate properly, especially in the early months of their business whilst they are establishing themselves and income is still growing. Once the franchisee is up and running they need to have sufficient Working Capital to run their business properly and spend money where necessary without having to wait for income to be generated from their customers. This may include paying staff and suppliers on time, or undertaking marketing activities. For this reason it is usual to stipulate a minimum level of Working Capital that franchisees require to start their business and also the minimum amount of Working Capital throughout the duration of their franchise.

Additional Costs:

Although many franchises are sold as turnkey businesses there may still be items of expenditure that are down to the franchisee to fund and purchase directly. These costs may include items such as their legal costs in having the Franchise Agreement professionally reviewed; there may be a premium the franchisee needs to pay on a particular commercial premises they want to operate from; it may be the requirement to have a vehicle for use within the business where a vehicle isn't included within the Set-Up Package; there may be costs relating to adapting/fitting out a room in the franchisees home where the franchise is designed to be run from. It is important that the prospective franchisee is aware of all the additional costs they may incur to ensure they have sufficient funds to meet them without compromising the operation of their business.

The Total Investment:

For most franchisees, the individual amounts of the Franchise Fee, the Set-Up Package, the Working Capital and any additional costs they may have, are less important than the Total Investment. Most franchisees are just concerned with how much the franchise will cost in total, so that they can arrange the necessary funds.

Sometimes franchisors try *not* to highlight all the costs as they want to appear cheaper than other competing franchises and they believe that under pricing the competition will make them more likely to recruit franchisees. It may be that by not marketing the true price they will attract more interest in their franchise however I believe that this approach is not only commercially dangerous as the franchisee will still need the full funds, but dangerous for the trust relationship between the franchisee and the franchisor. If the franchisor only reveals the true level of investment required later on in the recruitment process, the prospective franchisee may not be able to raise the additional funds and will have to pull out wasting both the franchisors and the prospective franchisees time. In addition, the loss of trust between prospective franchisee and franchisor at the outset is a recipe for future problems.

> *The loss of trust between prospective franchisee and franchisor at the outset is a recipe for future problems*

How to set the right price for the initial cost of the franchise:

Once there is clarity of what a franchisee will require to set-up and launch their franchise, it is possible to put a cost against this. Knowing how much it will cost the franchisor to provide everything the franchisee requires and how much help they need to launch their franchise, is the first step in setting the overall cost of the franchise.

Knowing the actual cost to the franchisor is only part of the equation when setting the price of the franchise. It is also important that the franchisor is also aware of the costs of other franchises that may be targeting the same profile of person as they are and what these competing franchises may be offering within their Franchise Set-Up Package.

The third factor when setting the franchise cost relates to the earning potential for the franchisee. Clearly one can charge more for a franchise where the franchisee will earn £100,000 per year compared with a franchise where they will only earn £20,000 a year.

The final consideration relates to brand perception. The franchisor needs to decide how they want to be perceived in the marketplace. If the franchised business sells expensive luxury goods, the franchisor may want to price their franchise higher than if they sold cheaper products, as this will reinforce their brand positioning as an up-market business.

Once the franchisor is aware of the actual cost to them for providing the franchisee with everything they will need to set-up and launch their franchise, knows what other competing franchises are charging, knows how much a franchisee is likely to earn, and why they want to position their franchise in the market, they are then in a position to set the franchise price.

There is no law or regulation in the UK that states what price a franchisor can charge for their franchise. Franchisors need to ensure that the franchise cost does not become a barrier to suitable people becoming their franchisees. As the franchisor will make the majority of their money from the ongoing fees charged and not the upfront cost, it is important that they recruit sufficient franchisees. Trying to make more money from the upfront cost at the expense of the number of franchisees recruited is a misguided strategy.

Payment Terms:

The final element related to setting the franchise price is to decide what payment terms will be operated. For the Franchise Fee, it is quite normal for franchisors to ask prospective franchisees to pay a deposit before release of the Franchise Agreement. This deposit shows commitment from the prospective franchisee so that the franchisor does not waste large amounts of time with individuals who are not really committed to becoming franchisees. In return for paying a deposit it is normal for a franchisor not to take any further enquiries for the territory under consideration whilst the prospective franchisee reviews the Franchise Agreement. If the franchisor is putting on hold any further enquiries for the territory under consideration it is usual for the franchisor to stipulate a timescale in which the prospective franchisee must make a decision, such as 30 days from receipt of the Franchise Agreement. Should a prospective franchisee decide, having reviewed the Franchise Agreement or for any other reason, that they are no longer interested in the franchise the usual practice is for the franchisor to return the deposit less any direct costs they have incurred. The British Franchise Associations rules state:

> "Pre-contract deposits must be refunded to prospective franchisees that (regardless of reason) withdraw their application, less any direct costs, and as actually incurred. Costs that, if related to the particular candidate can legitimately be deducted from any refund include, but are not necessarily limited to: Solicitors, Accountants, Travel Costs, Food and accommodation, Paid research for the particular territory. Costs that cannot be legitimately deducted include but are not limited to: Opportunity costs e.g. the cost of a lost sale, staff costs."

Where the franchise does go ahead however, it is normal that the balance of the Franchisee Fee (Franchise Fee less deposit) is paid at the time the Franchise Agreement is signed.

With regards payment of the Franchisee Set-Up Package different franchisors choose different payment models. Some franchisors ask for the Set-Up Package to be paid in full at the time of signing the Franchise Agreement. Other franchisors ask for the Set-Up Package to be paid before the start of the franchisees training. Some franchisors ask for some of the Set-Up Package to be paid at the time the Franchise Agreement is signed with the balance a set time before the franchisees training or when their will be direct costs such as fitting out the franchisees premises. The choice comes down to how long after signing the Franchise Agreement the franchisees training will commence. Some franchisors only run franchisee training courses at specific times of the year. For franchises that require premises, there can be a long delay whilst suitable premises are found and leases arranged. In this type of franchise I believe it can be unreasonable to expect a franchisee to pay the Franchise Set-Up Package in full and have the franchisor sit on the funds for long periods of time.

Where payment terms are staggered it is important to ensure that the franchisee still has all the funds available to them and that they are not hoping to use the gaps in the payment terms to try and source the additional funding.

In recent times, given the economic climate and the difficulty some prospective franchisees experience in raising finance, it has become more common for franchisors to offer staggered payment terms to ease the burden on the franchisee. I think this is commercially sensible however it is important that franchisors considering offering staggered payment terms should only do so in the right circumstances and to the right franchisee. Given that a franchisor makes the majority of their money from the ongoing success of their franchisees, I do not see any reason why a franchisor should not offer staggered payment terms instead of losing suitable prospective franchisees. I use the word suitable, because franchisors must be wary about offering prospective franchisees staggered payments where they are likely to always struggle with having sufficient funds to operate their franchise properly.

It has become more common for franchisors to offer staggered payment terms

If a franchisor does decide to offer staggered payments it is important to take legal advice as there are certain limits about the number of staggered payments one can take before coming under commercial lending legislation.

Ongoing Fees:
As previously stated, franchisors make their money from charging franchisees fees throughout the duration of the franchise. The four key types of ongoing fees are:

1. Franchise Management Fee
2. National Marketing Fee

69

3. Mark-Up on Products Supplied

4. Service Fees

1. The Franchise Management Fee, sometimes refereed to as a Royalty, is a charge made by the franchisor to cover their ongoing support to the franchisee and to generate a profit for the franchisor. There are normally two formats for the Franchise Management Fee, either a fixed monthly fee or a percentage of the franchisee's turnover. Where practical, my preference would be to link the Franchise Management Fee to a percentage of the franchisees income. This ensures that the franchisor has a vested interest in helping the franchisee to be successful otherwise the franchisors income will be affected. Some franchisors prefer to charge a fixed monthly fee. A fixed monthly fee is easier to manage and the franchisor does not have to rely on the franchisee declaring their monthly income to base their fee on. The downside to a fixed Management Fee, especially from the franchisees perspective, is that there is less incentive for a franchisor to help support a franchisee as they receive same amount of fees whatever they do. The percentage charged will vary dependent on the sector the franchise operates in and what is included within the Franchise Management Fee. Often a starting point when considering the viability of franchising from the franchisors perspective is to take ten percent of the franchisees income as the Franchise Management Fee. Fast food franchises however typically

charge in the region of five percent of income whereas some service franchises charge fifteen to twenty percent. It is therefore critical to set the Franchise Management Fee based on the services the franchisor will provide, what competing franchises are charging, and where the income generated from the Franchisor Management Fee makes franchising viable for both the franchisor and the franchisees.

Often franchisors that charge a fixed fee justify their decision to prospective franchisees by saying that the franchisee doesn't have to pay any more as the franchisee increases their level of turnover. This may seem attractive however on the flip side the franchisee stills has to pay the same fee even if their income reduces. There are instances where franchisees on a fixed monthly fee do not generate sufficient income to even pay the fixed monthly fee!

2. A National Marketing Fee is quite normal in franchising. This works on the principal that some marketing media are national and therefore why should one franchisee pay to market themselves in national media that will benefit others franchisees in the network. Therefore a national marketing fee is levied whereby all franchisees are charged a small amount each month and the franchisor uses these fees to undertake marketing for the benefit of the whole network. On television, one sees a number of franchises

that advertise their products or services such as McDonalds, Subway and Cash Generator. It would not be financially viable for any one franchisee to have to pay for advertising on television when this could benefit the whole network. Therefore having all franchisees contributing a small amount to a national marketing fund that will allow the franchisor to pay for television advertising makes more sense and benefits the whole franchise network.

3. Where a franchisor sells products to the franchisee, it is normal for the franchisor to make a mark-up on the cost to the franchisee. The franchisor should be able, due to the bulk buying ability or reduced in-house manufacturing costs, to mark-up the products they sell their franchisees and these products still be cheaper than the franchisees could purchase themselves. Problems occur with product mark-ups where the franchisee is forced to purchase products from the franchisor although they could buy the exact same product cheaper elsewhere. This leads to a feeling of bad will throughout the franchisee network and not surprisingly incidents of franchisees buying products elsewhere despite what the Operations Manual and the Franchise Agreement may say.

4. Where a franchisor provides services to the franchisee, such as staff payroll, customer invoice issuing and collection, or bookkeeping, the franchisor normally charges the

franchisee for these services. The same issue relates to services provided to the franchisee as it does to mark-up on products. So long as the identical services provided by the franchisor cannot be purchased cheaper elsewhere, problems are unlikely to occur.

How to set the right price for the ongoing fees:

As with the franchise cost there are a number of key factors that affect the ongoing fees charged and these are: knowing the actual cost to the franchisor in providing support and the central services provided to the franchisee; being aware of what competing franchises charge as ongoing fees, and calculating the effect of the ongoing fees on the profitability for both the franchisor and the franchisee.

It is important that the ongoing fees charged are seen as reasonable by the franchisee when compared against what they get for the fees paid and also compared with what other competing franchises charge. More importantly however is that the ongoing fees charged must allow the

The ongoing fees charged must allow the franchisee to make sufficient profit for the work they do

franchisee to make sufficient profit for the work they do and the income generated from the ongoing fees are sufficient to make franchising a business a financially viable proposition for the franchisor.

How to you set the right price to buy a franchise:

Setting the price for a franchise is based on five key elements: 1) a relatively low cost for granting the right to be a franchisee 2) the actual cost to the franchisor in providing the franchise set-up package; 3) being aware of the costs of other competing franchises; 4) the earning potential for the franchisee; 5) brand positioning and perception. There are many franchises where the total investment is less than £10,000 and a number with a total investment in excess of £100,000. It is up to each individual franchisor to use the five key elements to set the price which is right for their franchise.

QUESTION 5

HOW DO YOU DECIDE ON THE SIZE OF EACH TERRITORY WHEN FRANCHISING?

By Clive Sawyer, Managing Director, Business Options

Franchise Territory Mapping

The majority of franchises in the UK operate on an exclusive territory basis. This means that every franchisee will be given a map showing an area where they will be the only franchisee allowed to market their business within. I specifically said market their business rather than operate or sell because UK law allows customers to choose who they want to do business with. Therefore a customer based in one franchise territory can choose to do business with a franchisee in a different territory. What is permissible, in relationship to exclusive territories, is to prevent other franchisees from proactively marketing outside their territory. This provides a franchisee with the comfort that they will be able to develop and grow their business, within their territory, without direct competition from other franchisees in their network. Where a franchise model is based upon exclusive territories, it

75

is important to ensure that the criteria used to define the territories are based upon the key influencing factors for the business. The most common influencing factor is having sufficient potential customers in an area. For a lawn care franchise, one criteria used to define a territory is likely to be based on each territory having a minimum number of properties

The most common influencing factor is having sufficient potential customers in an area

with lawns. It is no good basing a lawn care territory just on population or number of homes, as this does not take into account areas that have a high proportion of homes without gardens such as flats and town houses, and areas with a higher average number of people living in each property. If a business is successful based on having a certain number of potential customers in its catchment area, then every franchise territory should have the same number of potential customers in their territory, if they are going to replicate the success of the business.

Having defined the franchise territory criteria a decision has to be made as to whether to map out the country in advance, predefining each franchise territory or creating individual territories only when a provisional franchise offer is made. The decision is normally down to the total number of potential franchise territories and whether the business will be franchising nationwide or only in specific geographic areas. If a business is only looking to have a few franchisees, it may be sensible to split the country into the specific number of predefined territories. Equally if a business is only going to franchise in certain geographic areas, such as major cities, then again it may make sense to predefine the franchise territories. However if a business is looking to recruit large numbers of franchisees across the whole country then it may be more sensible, at least at the start, not to predefine territories.

The problem with predefining territories is that it is very likely that prospective franchisees will not be based in the optimum location to maximise the potential of their franchise territory. Predefining territories can give rise to prospective franchisees being based on the border of two or even three predefined territories which will inevitably having an impact on their business, given that they can not proactively market outside their own territory. Customers may not want to travel from one side of a territory to the other, preferring to use another rival company that is closer by. If the franchisee has to deliver products to customers, it may be logistically harder and more costly to do so if they are based on the edge of their territory rather than being at its centre. It may also be that two franchisees in neighbouring territories are based very close together which may mean that they end up competing for business around where they are both based and lose out on business in other parts of their territories.

It is for these reasons that many businesses when they start franchising, choose not to predefine their territories. Business owners often worry, that if they do not predefine territories, how do they respond when a prospective franchisee enquiries about a territory. However this should not be a concern as the business owner will have set the criteria for their territories and can therefore inform prospective franchisees of this. The geographic size of a territory should have little bearing on the success of a franchise, having the right number of potential customers is what is important.

Another benefit of not having predefined territory boundaries is that it allows the franchisor to construct a territory for optimum performance based on where the franchisee is based. It may be that having a franchisee located in the centre of a territory is best for the franchisee and their customers. By not having predefined the territory it provides the franchisor the opportunity to create a bespoke territory with the right number of potential customers and with the franchisee based in the optimum location within the territory.

When a business starts franchising it is imperative, for the long term future of the franchise, that the first franchisees are successful. These first few franchisees will be the benchmark against which other prospective franchisees will evaluate the franchise against. If a franchisee underperforms, it can have a major impact on future franchisee recruitment as it will make it harder to substantiate any franchisee projections. Even if a prospective franchisee does not view this as an issue, they may find it harder to access funding from a Bank or investor as these institutions are likely to base their lending decision more on how the existing franchisee network is performing rather than the projections of a prospective franchisee.

One of the largest concerns businesses have with building territories around franchisees rather than predefining territories, is that the franchisor can be left with areas between existing territories that they cannot sell, because they do not meet the minimum criteria required for the territory. This is a valid concern, however before making a decision over which approach to take, one should consider how realistic it is that the business will sell franchisees in absolutely every possible location. For many franchisors, it is very unlikely that they will sell franchises in every conceivable territory, and therefore it makes better commercial sense to have the franchisees in the territories they do sell, performing really well, compared with having more potential franchise territories but with the franchisees performing less well.

As with most things, there is of course a compromise when considering these two approaches. A franchisor can start by not predefining territories to give the first franchisees the best chance of success and then once they have recruited a certain number of franchisees, they can choose to predefine the remaining areas into territories, allowing them to maximise the potential remaining number of franchises they can offer.

When defining territories I have encountered the misconception on behalf of franchisors that it isn't critical to get the territory criteria right at the outset as it can always be changed at a later date. Technically this is correct as it is possible to change predefined territories however changing territories once sold is very problematic.

When a franchisee signs the Franchise Agreement, the Franchise Agreement will state the territory boundaries. As the Franchise Agreement is a legally binding document for both the franchisee and the franchisor changing any part of it requires agreement from both parties. If a franchisor wants to increase the size of a franchisees territory there may be little objection from the franchisee, however reducing the size of a franchisees territories is very likely to lead to serious objections. The other major consideration when considering altering existing territories is that any actual franchisee trading projections will become meaningless to future potential franchisees as they will have been achieved on different territory criteria that new franchisees will operate under. Franchisors should spend the time at the outset to get the territory criteria right before they start franchising and only in exceptional circumstances should consider changing them.

Whichever approach a business takes to creating franchise territories, the most critical aspect is to base the territory on the key influencing factors for the business. It is essential that all franchisees have sufficient potential customers in their territory to enable them to generate the level of business required to be successful.

> *It is essential that all franchisees have sufficient potential customers in their territory*

How to decide on the size of each franchise territory:

This is only relevant when franchise territories are offered on an exclusive basis. Where this is the case the golden rule is to base the franchise territory size upon the key influencing factors for the business. The most common influencing success factor for virtually every business is having sufficient potential customers. If a business is successful based on having a certain number of potential customers in its catchment area, then every franchise territory should have the same number of potential customers in their territory, if they are going to replicate the success of the business. Therefore the criteria for franchise territories will be different for each business based on their customer profile.

IS THE FRANCHISOR LIABLE FOR THE ACTIONS OF ITS FRANCHISEES?

By Nicola Broadhurst, Partner, Stevens & Bolton LLP

Whether a franchisor can be held responsible by a third party for the acts and failures of its franchisees depends on the extent of control that the franchisor exercises over its franchisees' businesses. In a true business format franchise the franchisor should not be liable for its franchisee's actions and this is a key distinguishing feature of

> *The franchisor should not be liable for its franchisee's actions*

franchising as a method of business expansion when compared to certain other structures. A franchise is sold on the basis that a franchisee is a business owner in his own right operating his own independent business, albeit under the relevant controls of the franchise system. It is this separation of liability that makes franchising an attractive proposition for a business owner, who will usually be keen to distance itself from its franchisee's business. Sometimes however the lines get blurred and as franchisors are inevitably seen as having deeper pockets than franchisees customers are only too keen to try to establish a cause of action against the franchisor to claim recompense for loss suffered.

Most franchise agreements will go to some length to emphasise the independence of the franchised business stating that the franchisee is not a partner, agent, or employee of the franchisor. Despite such statements however, there may well be circumstances where a franchisor is potentially liable and in nearly every case such liability rests on how much control the franchisor actually exerted over the franchisee in practice. It is a basic premise of franchising that the franchisor must retain some control over the use of its name, goods or services, but the extent of this control must be carefully considered. No matter what an agreement says, the true nature of the franchise working relationship will be scrutinised to see if it goes beyond that stated in the agreement.

The main ways in which a franchisor can be liable for its franchisee's actions are discussed below.

Agency

(i) Actual authority

A franchisor will be liable for the actions of its franchisee where the franchisee had "actual" authority to bind the franchisor and was acting as the franchisor's agent. If a customer who suffers loss as a result of a franchisee's action or mistake could successfully establish that the franchisee was acting with the authority of the franchisor at the time of the loss then the franchisor will be liable. Clearly this is not always easy to prove and generally in the normal course of operating a franchise a franchisee will not be seen as the franchisor's agent and will not be permitted to hold himself out as one either. The test for liability in these circumstances will depend on the level of control exercised by the franchisor over the franchisee in operating his business. In Allergy Care (Testing) Ltd v Customs & Excise Commissioners (2003), the fact that an upfront fee and ongoing fees were paid by franchisees in consideration for services being provided by the franchisor was an influential factor in determining that the relationship was sufficiently independent. Although this case concerned VAT assessment and whether the two businesses in question were separate taxable entities with a normal commercial relationship at sufficient arms length, it is likely that similar principles and reasoning would be followed in other cases.

(ii) Apparent authority

Even where a true agency relationship does not exist between the franchisor and franchisee a third party can still hold the franchisor liable under the doctrine of agency by estoppel if he can show that the franchisee was acting with the "apparent" authority of the franchisor.

A third party can still hold the franchisor liable under the doctrine of agency by estoppel

Under the doctrine if the third party can establish that due to the franchisor's actions he believed the franchisee was authorised to act on behalf of the franchisor and as a result he entered into the transaction with the franchisee, the franchisor will be prevented from denying the franchisee's agency and will be liable for any of the franchisee's acts or omissions.

In order for this argument to be successful the franchisor must be shown to have taken some action which misled the third party, for example, a representation. A franchisor therefore needs to be extremely cautious about any statements that it makes.

It is arguable, however, that the use of the franchisor's intellectual property and trade name is in itself sufficient to create an agency by estoppel. With many franchise outlets the public are usually completely unaware that they are operated under franchise and assume that they are all part of the same trading entity. This point has, however yet to be definitively decided by the English courts.

This is an area of liability often ignored by franchisors. It is particularly relevant where the franchisor negotiates large contracts in its own name on behalf of the franchise network and then authorises or sub-contracts the work to its franchisees; or

it offers a central booking service for its franchisees' customers. Here the franchisor will handle all enquiries and secure contracts with customers for services or products which the franchisee is meant to perform or provide.

Where a franchisor has agreed terms and even pricing with a customer it is easy to see how the customer might consider the franchisee to simply be an agent of the franchisor, particularly where the invoicing is done by the franchisor on behalf of the franchisee and payment collected centrally by the franchisor.

If the franchisee, during the course of performing the contract, caused damage or loss to the customer, the customer could well have a claim against the franchisor in these circumstances. The relationship between the franchisor and the franchisee needs to be clearly stated at the outset and brought to the attention of the customer.

In these situations the franchisor should tell the customer in what capacity it and the franchisee are acting. For example the customer should be told that the franchisor is only acting on behalf of the franchisee and that it will be the franchisee who will fulfil the contract. The franchisor's staff should be trained to explain this when taking any calls from prospective customers and the terms and conditions provided to a customer or on the franchisor's web site should back this up. The franchise agreement should also make it clear that the franchisor is only acting in the capacity of the franchisee's agent in securing such contracts thereby making the franchisee liable to the customer.

Vicarious liability

It is well established that an employer can be vicariously liable for the acts or omissions of its employees during the course of the employment; can a franchisor be liable in a similar fashion? Provided the franchise transaction is structured appropriately so it is not a contract of service, a franchisee should not be deemed to be an employee of the franchisor and this issue should not arise. The key factors in determining the relationship are: whether the franchisee bears the risk of loss as well as profit, whether the franchisee receives a wage from the franchisor and the extent to which the franchisee is free to operate the business.

Although most franchise agreements stipulate plenty of general quality controls it should still leave the franchisee free to comply with those controls in the time, manner and method in which he sees fit. However where a franchisee relies solely on the performance of national contracts secured by the franchisor and performs very little if any other work for other customers, then there may well be a case to argue that the franchisee is no more than an employee or worker. If this were the case the franchisor could again be responsible for any act or omission of the franchisee which caused any third party loss whilst that franchisee was performing the work.

Partnership

A franchisee can bind the franchisor by his actions if the franchise relationship is in fact found to be a partnership in the true legal meaning of that word. Partnership is defined by Section 1 of the Partnership Act 1890 as "the relationship which subsists between persons carrying on a business in common with a view to profit". The Act also sets out various rules to determine whether a partnership exists, mainly centring on whether the actual profits of the business are shared. This is the main distinguishing factor between partnerships and franchises.

Whilst most franchisors charge a management fee based on franchisee's turnover, it is unusual for a franchisor to share profits with a franchisee and unlikely therefore that a franchise agreement will evidence a partnership. Significantly the franchisor must have knowingly allowed itself to be held out as a partner of the franchisee and this would be extremely rare. The third party would also have to show that he relied on this relationship in entering into the transaction.

Negligence

A franchisor could potentially be liable for the loss suffered by its franchisee's customer if it could be successfully proven that the franchisor owed a duty of care to that customer and was negligent. This would be difficult. Firstly, a duty of care must be established and, depending on the circumstances, it is unlikely that a sufficiently close relationship between the franchisor and the customer existed. Even where a duty of care is established, the type of loss that could be recovered is limited.

A franchisor could be liable under statute where the products that it supplied to its franchisees for onward sale under the franchisor's trade name or trade mark to customers were found to be defective. Depending on whether the products were actually manufactured by the franchisor it may have recourse in turn to the manufacturer if this is the case.

What can a franchisor do?

It is a harsh fact that someone who has suffered loss will usually look to the party with the deepest pockets when bringing an action and franchisors will often be seen as a likely target. Therefore a franchisor should take as many precautions as possible.

(i) Insurance

Perhaps obviously the franchisor can seek to put in place adequate insurance against all risks including the risk of being sued by a third party or even its own

> *Someone who has suffered loss will usually look to the party with the deepest pockets when bringing an action*

franchisees. There are a number of specialist insurance packages on offer which are tailored specifically for franchisors to help protect against costly claims.

(ii) Drafting the franchise agreement appropriately

The franchise agreement should contain all relevant disclaimers and expressly state that no agency, employee or partnership relationship exists between the franchisor and the franchisee. There should be no other provisions in the agreement which could contradict these statements.

Where the franchisor is offering assistance with the franchisee's customers whether by providing back office support, securing work or processing payments the capacity in which the franchisor is acting should always be stated.

As most potential claims that a franchisor may suffer from third parties in respect of its franchisee's actions or failures will be from the franchisee's customers and suppliers it makes sense for the franchise agreement to try to impose certain controls on the way in which the franchisee must behave in the business to prevent such claims arising in the first place. Typically therefore the franchise agreement will contain a number of stipulations some of which are set out below.

Creditors

The franchisee should be required to pay all creditors of the business. This will include the franchisee's suppliers who may have a good relationship with the franchisor which could be jeopardised if the franchisee fails to pay or is consistently late in paying.

Customer documentation

The franchisor should provide the franchisee with the standard terms and conditions to use with the franchisee's customers and the franchisee should not be permitted to change these without the franchisor's consent.

This allows the franchisor to ensure that the terms and conditions that a customer signs explains the relationship between the franchisor and the franchisee so that there is no confusion in the future and states that the franchisee is responsible for the work to be done and that the franchisor has no liability in this regard. At the very least this may deter would be claimants. This is of course not so easy with large national accounts where the work has been sub-contracted to the franchisee to perform. It is surprising however how many franchisors overlook this area and the chance to further protect its position.

Customer complaints procedure

The franchisor should require the franchisee to notify the franchisor of any complaint which cannot be settled within 48 hours (sometimes longer can be given) and reserve the right to step in and take over the handling of the complaint or at least require the franchisee to follow the franchisor's instructions. Usually the franchisor has far more experience in dealing with complaints and will be more effective at damage control than a franchisee. It would also be sensible for the franchisor to have a customer complaint and refund procedure in its operations manual to assist its franchisees in this area.

Strict controls should be placed on the way in which the franchisee can use the trade marks. Where the franchisee is a limited liability company it should be prevented from using the trade mark in its corporate name to minimise public misconception about the relationship between the franchisee and the franchisor. Where the franchised business is operating from commercial premises the franchisee must be required to display clear notices to the public stating that the franchised business is a separate and independent business and operated under franchise.

Indemnity

The franchisee should be required to indemnify the franchisor against all loss and liability suffered as a result of the franchisee's action and if possible to extend this indemnity to cover the actions of the franchisee's employees and customers. Therefore if the franchisor incurs costs defending a claim brought by a customer of the franchisee or any other third party as a result of something the franchisee did or failed to do it at least has a right of recourse to recover such costs from the franchisee. Ideally the indemnity should cover all actions or omissions of the franchisee and not just negligent acts or omissions. This therefore allows the franchisor to recover its costs where it has had to deal with a complaint from one of the franchisee's customers which was groundless.

This is a strong protection for the franchisor. An indemnity allows the franchisor to recover pound for pound all losses, costs and expenses

An indemnity allows the franchisor to recover pound for pound all losses, costs and expenses

that it has drafted for in the wording of the indemnity without much wriggle room for the franchisee.

(iii) Public facing material

Where possible all advertising and marketing material used by the franchisee should state the nature of the franchise relationship even down to the compliment slips. The material can proudly display the trade mark but somewhere on the document should be the franchisee's name and address and preferably the fact that it is a franchisee of the franchisor.

All invoices and contract documentation provided to the customer should state the franchisee's name and address and the capacity in which it is acting i.e. as a franchisee. This all provides ammunition to a franchisor keen to rebut a third party's claim that somehow the franchisor is liable for its franchisee's actions.

Reality check

Ultimately however, whether or not a franchisor is liable in law for its franchisee's actions, in reality it will always suffer and have to take some form of responsibility where a franchisee's act or omission harms another or causes bad publicity. The franchisor's brand, reputation and goodwill is always on the line once a franchise is granted, this is a risk of relinquishing control over a brand and an inherent risk in franchising. No matter what the franchise agreement says it is always a question of enforcement and consistent monitoring to ensure standards are maintained and required actions are taken. This should always be part of a franchisor's risk management so that it is easily able to spot a franchisee that is not up to the requisite standard and offer re-training or more closely monitor the franchisee to prevent issues arising in the future.

> *The franchisor's brand, reputation and goodwill is always on the line*

WHY HAVE A FRANCHISE CONTRACT?

By Nicola Broadhurst, Partner, Stevens & Bolton LLP

Unlike many other countries, the UK does not have franchise specific legislation. Without the comfort of having certain rights enshrined in statute which can be relied on in the absence of a written agreement the need for a Franchisor to have a well drafted and comprehensive franchise agreement becomes essential. The agreement is probably the most important document in the transaction process as it governs the franchise relationship. The more detailed it is the better to provide certainty and avoid arguments. As a result a franchise agreement can be extremely lengthy as it attempts to cover all angles for the Franchisor and still offer a fair deal to the franchisee.

The need for franchise legislation has been debated over the years but has been consistently resisted on the basis that existing legislation and case law which impacts commercial contracts is sufficient. To a large extent this is correct and regard must be had to the Unfair Contract Terms Act 1977 when

The need for franchise legislation has been debated over the years

dealing with any attempts to exclude or limit the Franchisor's liability to its Franchisees and also competition law both at national and EC levels.

In addition, the structure of many franchise networks could be construed as pyramid schemes or agency arrangements and care must be taken to ensure that this is avoided. The consequences for ignoring relevant legislation can be disastrous for a Franchisor, ranging from a fine to rendering the entire franchise agreement unenforceable and in the case of pyramid selling schemes, a criminal offence.

The British Franchise Association has adopted the European Franchise Federation's Code of Ethics and published a best practice guide called The Ethics of Franchising. As this is the only best practice guide regularly being followed by Franchisors in the UK, it stands to reason that whether or not a Franchisor wishes to be a member of the BFA its agreement should be drafted in line with the BFA's Code of Ethics to ensure best practice is being followed.

Main aims of the Franchise Agreement:

A franchise agreement should do the following:-

(i) detail the rights and obligations of the Franchisor and the Franchisee in all key areas of the franchised business;

(ii) protect the Franchisor's intellectual property, trade secrets, reputation and business interests;

(iii) detail the rules governing the operation of the franchised business. These will be supplemented by the Franchisor's operations manual which works alongside the agreement;

(iv) impress upon a prospective Franchisee the seriousness of the undertaking and the commitment required to help avoid time wasters; and

(v) act as a marketing tool by demonstrating the commitment of the Franchisor in investing in a well drafted, comprehensive agreement.

Once the agreement has been signed its terms will be enforced, even if they prove more onerous than originally intended or anticipated unless a successful legal challenge can be brought.

There may be scope to challenge certain terms of the agreement under the Unfair Contract Terms Act 1977 but such challenges are fairly limited in nature. The most usual challenge is where the Franchisee alleges a serious misrepresentation on the part of the Franchisor. Therefore as part of a general risk management policy, a Franchisor must ensure that all pre-contract representations, statements and promises are clearly documented and cab be substantiated to avoid unwelcome allegations at a later date.

Uniformity of Terms:

Although a franchise agreement is a commercial contract, it is usually issued as a non-negotiable agreement. This makes it significantly different from many other commercial agreements which are usually open for negotiation but this approach is justifiable. A Franchisor should be contracting with each franchisee on the same basis and same terms to ensure that all are treated equally and fairly. This principle of fairness is one of the key tenets of the Code of Ethics. There is nothing more likely to cause discontent within a franchised network than for one Franchisee to discover that another is being treated more favourably. It is human nature to gossip and no matter how well a Franchisor thinks that variations will be kept

> *There is nothing more likely to cause discontent within a franchised network than for one Franchisee to discover that another is being treated more favourably*

secret, these have a tendency to be discovered. Sometimes there are good commercial reasons for agreeing a variation, but these should be avoided wherever possible. Consistency promotes certainty and equality.

One-sided franchise agreements:

Franchise agreements are weighted heavily in favour of the Franchisor as it is the Franchisor's intellectual property and brand that is being put at risk when it relinquishes control and permits replication of its business. Again the one-sided nature of franchise agreements tends to shock prospective franchisees and those lawyers not familiar with franchising. Provided the agreement has been drafted in line with the Code of Ethics and the Franchisor commits to acting fairly and reasonably towards a franchisee then such one sidedness is acceptable. But without legislative checks there will always be the temptation for a Franchisor to push the boundaries beyond what would be considered reasonable particularly where a franchisee is not appropriately advised.

Key Elements of the Franchise Agreement:

Although every franchise agreement should be tailored for a franchise concept, there is a general format that is followed in ethical business format franchising and which encapsulates the key principles of the BFA's Code of Ethics. This has resulted in fairly standardised franchise agreements contained certain key elements discussed below.

Introduction:

The background to the franchise agreement is usually set out in what lawyers call "recitals". These should detail the context of the agreement, who owns the intellectual property and the grant of rights. The ownership of the intellectual property is important as the Franchisor must have the right to use and sub-licence the use of the brand and other intellectual property. Many business owners establish a new company to franchise the business concept, this ring-fences the liability of the franchise business from the core business which may continue trading separately. The new company will not usually own the intellectual property as this remains with the core business but it should be licensed by the core business to use this.

Rights Granted:

The right to operate a franchise is always granted, never sold and a franchisee operates the business with consent from the Franchisor but never actually owns the trade mark and other intellectual property. This should not prevent a franchisee selling the branded business, but it may only do so with the Franchisor's consent. On expiry or termination (without an onwards sale) of the agreement, all rights to the franchise will revert back to the Franchisor.

The grant of rights should state whether the Franchisee is being given an exclusive, sole or non-exclusive right to trade, usually within a designated area. Sole rights means that the Franchisor will not appoint another third party within that area, but does not prevent the Franchisor from trading itself. Where a Franchisee has exclusive rights, the Franchisor is prevented from operating in that area either directly or through another. It is usual for exclusive areas to be given as it is easier to sell a franchise on this basis to a prospective franchisee.

Term of the Franchise:
The grant of the franchise is usually for a specific period of time of not less than five years and sometimes ten years. The initial term must be long enough to allow a Franchisee to recoup his capital investment and realise at least two years profit.

An initial term of more than ten years is not advisable as the franchise concept will no doubt develop in ways which would justify changes to the agreement or an increase in fees. It would nearly impossible to legislate for all these changes in the agreement; therefore there should be a convenient break at which the Franchisee can be required to sign up to the then current form of franchise agreement. This also promotes uniformity of contractual terms across the network.

Care is required where the agreement requires the Franchisee to buy all of its product requirements from the Franchisor as a term of more than five years may well infringe relevant competition law.

Renewal:

Most franchise agreements allow the Franchisee the option to renew, but this is not obligatory under the Code of Ethics. If a Franchisee is performing well there should be little reason not to renew although some Franchisors believe that new blood is required as franchisees reach their comfort zone. Renewal also provides the Franchisor with the opportunity to require the Franchisee to sign up to the then current form of franchise agreement and impose higher fees.

The right to renew tends to be conditional. Franchisees must serve notice to renew within specific time limits, usually six months before expiry to allow the Franchisor to plan ahead. It is also common for additional conditions to be fulfilled before renewal is granted, such as re-vamping the business to current standards, waiving claims against the Franchisor and paying the Franchisor's costs. A failure to satisfy a condition can result in renewal being forfeit. Difficulties arise where both parties forget that the agreement has expired and continue to trade. Essentially they are trading on the terms of the expired agreement which is implied into their relationship but issues occur where a Franchisor then wishes to terminate and impose restrictive covenants on the Franchisee.

Franchisor's Contractual Obligations:

The Franchisor's obligations tend to be divided into its initial obligations and continuing obligations. A Franchisor cannot simply impose numerous obligations on the Franchisee whilst accepting few, if any, obligations itself. In ethical franchising, support by a Franchisor is not an optional extra and must be provided. The obligations should be clearly and unambiguously set out, not simply cross referred to in the operations manual as the manual can subsequently be changed by the Franchisor without the Franchisee's consent.

> *In ethical franchising, support by a Franchisor is not an optional extra and must be provided*

The Franchisor's initial responsibilities should include: assisting the Franchisee to open for the business, providing initial training and a copy of the operations manual on loan, together with any other initial support services which may have promised to the Franchisee.

On a continuing basis the Franchisor should commit to providing advice and support to its Franchisees. Lack of support is one of the most common complaints raised by franchisees, particularly those who are failing. The Franchisor must be prepared to have dedicated personnel to provide such support as the network grows and be accessible at all times during business hours to its Franchisees.

Operations Manual:

The operations manual contains the daily operational details of the franchised business. A well drafted operations manual is one which not only supplements the franchise agreement but should provide all the detailed know how that a Franchisee with no previous experience would need to know in order to run the business. Most business format franchises are heavily dependent on the use of operation manuals and it is the Franchisor's obligation to provide those to its Franchisees at the outset and to ensure it is regularly updated to reflect changes and business practices. It forms part of the agreement and Franchisees are usually obliged to strictly comply with its provisions.

A Franchisor should have the right to unilaterally amend the manual and impose such changes on the Franchisee without consent. It is vital if a franchised business is to develop and adapt over the course of the initial term, that the Franchisor can introduce some modifications (within reason) on the Franchisee in order to maintain uniformity and adapt to market conditions quickly and effectively. These modifications however should not materially change the rights granted in the agreement and it is easy to see how this can be abused. Therefore, the franchise agreement should provide that if there is a conflict between the agreement and the manual, the agreement will prevail, as it is this document that the Franchisees will have had an opportunity to take legal advice on. A Franchisee should not be given a copy of the operations manual prior to signing the franchise agreement as it will contain confidential information but should be provided with an opportunity to review this at head office.

> *A Franchisee should not be given a copy of the operations manual prior to signing the franchise agreement*

Franchisee's Contractual Obligations:

The agreement usually contains lengthy obligations on the part of the Franchisee. The main obligations include observing minimum operating hours, paying the franchise fee on time and without deductions, following the accounting system laid down by the Franchisor, maintaining the requisite insurance coverage, allowing the Franchisor's staff to inspect the premises and speak to customers to establish that standards are being maintained, and to purchase goods or products from the Franchisor or its designated suppliers.

Where a Franchisee has been granted an exclusive territory it will usually be prevented from actively selling into other territories. Care must be taken however as an absolute ban on the Franchisee's ability to respond to unsolicited enquiries received from outside his territory could be constitute a breach of competition law and be potentially unenforceable.

Payment Provisions:

Usually there is a separate section in the agreement which deals with the fees that a Franchisee is required to pay. The manner and timing of such payments should be clearly set. Generally a Franchisee will have to pay an initial franchise fee to secure the grant of rights and then a monthly (sometimes quarterly) management service fee and possibly an advertising fee.

(i) Initial Franchise Fees:

The levels of initial franchise fees vary dramatically but should be capable of being broken down and justified by the Franchisor. The initial fee should reflect the actual set up costs to the Franchisor of granting a franchise with a very small element of profit unless the brand is a super brand or well established.

(ii) Management Service Fee

The management service fee can be a fixed fee but is more usually calculated as a percentage of the total turnover achieved by a Franchisee after deducting VAT. Again, the percentage does vary but there are industry norms in each market sector which should be considered by the Franchisor and its advisors. The disadvantage of fixed fees is that they can penalise a struggling Franchisee, although where a Franchisee is incredibly successful, the fixed fee can often be modest when compared to a percentage. A management service fee which is a percentage with a minimum fixed fee as a fall back option is, for a Franchisor, the best of both worlds, but from a Franchisee's point of view is

> *The disadvantage of fixed fees is that they can penalise a struggling Franchisee*

less attractive as the Franchisor is always making money regardless of the success of the Franchisee's business. The fairest fee is probably the simple percentage as a Franchisor only makes money when a Franchisee is succeeding which inevitably encourages a greater level of support by the Franchisor.

(iii) Advertising Fee

Franchisors often also require franchisees to pay an advertising fee which is held in a central fund, again this is usually a percentage of the Franchisee's turnover. Advertising fees can be a contentious area of the franchise agreement. A very successful Franchisee may feel that he is subsidising others where the advertising fee is a percentage of his revenues. This is an area which can be subject to some negotiations and often a reduction in an advertising fee can be offered as an incentive for a high achieving Franchisee.

Advertising:

The franchise agreement should restrict the way in which a Franchisee can advertise the business in order to protect the brand. Inappropriate advertising can easily damage the reputation of the business. In some contracts there is an obligation on Franchisees to commit to a minimum spend on advertising, or to contribute regularly to an advertising fund which is maintained by the Franchisor to promote the network. Where a central fund is maintained by the Franchisor, there should be some accountability as to how it uses the money and a break down of the annual income and expenditure should be sent to Franchisee on request.

Sale, Death and Incapacity:

The ways in which a Franchisee can exit the franchise agreement should be covered. The most obvious exit route is a sale of the franchised business. As a purchaser will become a franchisee the Franchisor will want to approve him and therefore the agreement should prevent the Franchisee selling or assigning the business without the Franchisor's consent. Consent should be conditional on the purchaser satisfying the same rigorous selection procedure that other Franchisee had to undergo. In addition the Franchisor may want a right of first refusal to allow for a buy back of the business. The price offered however should be the same as that offered by the purchaser as a Franchisor should not undercut but the Franchisor can reserve the right to have the business valued.

The way in which the sale is dealt with will vary from franchise to franchise but most Franchisors seek to impose a transfer fee to recoup their administrative costs in investigating the purchaser plus a commission payment where it has introduced the purchaser. The levels of these fees vary but they must be reasonable and should not present an obstacle to the sale.

On the death of a Franchisee, the Franchisor should allow for a period of time within which the business can be dealt with by the personal representatives. Usually there is a short period of time within which the personal representatives can nominate a beneficiary who, after approval by the Franchisor can take over the business or a slightly longer period of time within which the business can be sold. The Franchisor should reserve the right to appoint a manager to maintain the goodwill in the business in the interim at the expense of the business. The time periods vary and depend on how long it will take before goodwill in the business starts diminishing.

Again, in the event of incapacity, the Franchisor may wish to reserve the right to appoint a manager but will still want to have the option to force the Franchisee to sell the business should the incapacity go on for too long. The length of period varies from anywhere between three days and one hundred and eighty days or more before which the business must be sold.

Minimum Performance Targets:

Most franchise agreements contain either key performance indicators or minimum performance targets which must be achieved by Franchisees in order to maintain the right to continue to trade. These are most common in franchise agreements where Franchisees have been granted an exclusive territory as a Franchisor will want the ability to step in if the territory is not being exploited by an underperforming Franchisee.

When the concept of minimum performance targets were first endorsed by the BFA it recommended that these should not be more than fifty percent of the projected financial income for the network if they were linked to achievement of revenue. Interestingly, the percentage was increased to seventy percent after consultation with a representative group of franchisees. Most Franchisees support such targets as they are perceived as promoting high standards across a franchise network. But minimum performance targets should be applied fairly with a staggered procedure to failure not simply termination for one incidence of failure.

A Franchisee's performance should be reviewed regularly, and in the event of failure the Franchisor should commit to working with the Franchisee to improve performance for a period of time. The Franchisor's right to terminate the agreement for a failure to achieve targets should only apply where it has provided assistance to a Franchisee and the failure has persisted.

Terminating the Agreement:

One of the key parts of the franchise agreement from the Franchisor's point of view will be its ability to terminate the agreement where the Franchisee is in breach. Most franchise agreements contain a lengthy list of those breaches which would justify termination of the agreement by the Franchisor. The usual breaches include: failure to pay fees on time, failure to provide accounting information, insolvency and any type of breach which would bring the trade name into disrepute. An ethical Franchisor should also provide for termination with a partial refund of the initial fee where a Franchisee does not pass the initial training. This allows the Franchisor to remove an unsuitable candidate with little harm done and softens the blow for the Franchisee.

Whilst a comprehensive list of breaches helps avoid arguments, unless it is a fundamental breach the Franchisor should be careful to allow the Franchisee a reasonable period of time to cure the breach. The courts expect parties in dispute should be seen to be attempting to resolve their differences before resorting to litigation and to act reasonably at all times. The courts also have a tendency to be predisposed to franchisees and find in their favour unless there was a compelling reason for the Franchisor's action.

Usually only the Franchisor has the contractual right to terminate whilst the Franchisee does not. This protects the Franchisor from a Franchisee from acquiring all its trade secrets and then terminating. The Franchisee does however always have a common law right

> *Usually only the Franchisor has the contractual right to terminate whilst the Franchisee does not*

to terminate the franchise agreement where the Franchisor is in fundamental breach of its obligations, but such breaches are often hard to prove.

Consequences of Termination:

On termination it is vital that the Franchisor ensures that the Franchisee is disassociated from the network as quickly as possible. The agreement should detail the actions a Franchisee must take on termination and should include: reserving the right to enter the Franchisee's place of business to take down

113

any relevant signs or advertising material, obtaining full lists of relevant customers and usually some form of restriction on the way in which the Franchisee can trade for a period of time after termination.

Restrictive Covenants:

On termination a Franchisor will want a breathing space to try to re-sell the area and protect the business that has been built up. Therefore restrictive covenants which prevent a franchisee from trading in a competing business for a period of time in the area and elsewhere are usually included. However as all such restrictions are on the face of them anti-competitive they are notoriously difficult to enforce and this is one of the most contentious areas of the agreement.

In order to enforce such restrictions the duration or geographical scope of the restrictions must be reasonable but there is no hard and fast rule as to what would be considered reasonable under relevant case law. Under the European block exemption regulation dealing with vertical agreements and which would apply to franchise agreements, a restriction of more than twelve months would be considered unreasonable. A restriction limited to the premises or the territory of the Franchisee concerned would probably be enforceable but an extension of the geographical scope outside this area would need to be considered carefully.

Buy Back Provisions:

Some franchise agreements, usually those with premise based Franchisees, include buy back provisions which apply on termination and allow the Franchisor to step in immediately and take over. This is a useful protection for Franchisors as it helps to preserve the goodwill in the business from day one and effectively ousts the Franchisee. The Franchisor must pay to take back the business but this is not an open market price. Instead the Franchisor will usually pay cost price or written down value for equipment and goods and nothing for goodwill on the basis that the Franchisee no longer had the right to trade the business as a going concern.

Entire Agreement Clauses:

Most franchise agreements will contains an entire agreement clause which states that the agreement and the operations manual constitute the entire agreement between the parties and replaces anything that went before. This is intended to protect the Franchisor against claims of misrepresentation based on something that was said or documented prior to the franchise agreement such as financial projections. Whilst largely effective such a provision does not offer complete protection. For example if financial projections bear no resemblance to what has been achieved in practice and the Franchisee relied on these when signing the agreement then the Franchisor may still face a claim for fraudulent misrepresentation. Such liability cannot be contractually excluded as a matter of law.

Conclusion:

The franchise agreement has to encompass numerous aspects of the franchise business and therefore it is no wonder that it can be a lengthy document. When disputes occur what is written in the franchise agreement will often determine the outcome and the costs involved in the matter. If the issue has not been dealt with adequately, then costs increase and aggravation soars. Prevention is always better than cure.

WHAT INTELLECTUAL PROPERTY RIGHTS ARE LIKELY TO BE INVOLVED WHEN FRANCHISING A BUSINESS AND HOW ARE SUCH RIGHTS PROTECTED?

By Jonathan Chadd, Partner, Leathes Prior Solicitors

At the core of any franchising arrangement is a licence of particular intellectual property rights. These commonly include the right to use a trading name and brand and the business system which has been developed and proven to work by the franchisor. The franchisees are licensed to use such rights in replicating the business model. Understanding the scope of such rights and how they may be protected is therefore of key importance to all franchisors.

Trade Marks:

The brand and/or trade name under which the business trades is both one of the principal features and benefits of a franchised business since it designates to the consumer the consistency and quality of the services or goods in respect of which it is used.

The trade name should therefore, where possible, be protected by registration as a trade mark. Whilst the franchisor will have common law rights in its unregistered trade marks, these are acquired by, and based upon, their prior use and have to be proven if challenged; whereas registration as a trade mark identifies to the world the trade mark owner's rights both to use and sub-licence the use of a mark to its franchisees.

A trade mark may either be a word mark, which gives the proprietor rights to the use of a word or words in any form or style, or it may be a logo or device, being a stylised form of the brand under which the goods and services are sold. Such a device may include words as well as pictures or symbols but the registered rights subsist in the logo or device as a whole and the right to use the words alone is not protected or exclusive to the trade mark owner.

A franchisor will need to consider carefully what mark, or marks, to register and in which classes (i.e. in respect of which products and services), who is to be the proprietor (registered owner) of the mark and whether to register it in the UK alone or to apply for a European Community Mark ("CTM") which will provide protection in twenty seven EU member states.

> *A franchisor will need to consider carefully what mark, or marks, to register and in which classes*

Registering in the UK is quicker and less expensive but if a franchisor is seriously contemplating expansion into the Republic of Ireland and other EU states then a CTM is very cost effective given the scope of protection it will secure.

If any party other than the franchisor company is to be the registered proprietor of the trade mark then there will need to be a simple trade mark licence concluded between that proprietor and the franchisor permitting, under a separate licence, the use of the mark by the franchisor and the right to sub licence its use to its franchisees. Securing proper advice on these issues at an early stage is vital for any prospective franchisor as part of the process of getting the structure of the business right at the outset.

Whether or not a trading name or mark is registered, the proprietor will have common law rights in it established through the use of the trade name or mark in connection with the operation of the business. Thus, any person who sets up a competing business using the same name or mark or one that is substantially similar may be restrained by the proprietor of the original mark bringing an action for "passing off" under common law. This requires a demonstration by the proprietor of his prior use rights in the mark or trading name and he will need to show that the alleged infringing trading name or mark is so similar as to cause confusion among consumers. Taking such steps is both time consuming and expensive (as well as uncertain). It is very much quicker and simpler if the franchisor has a registered trade mark and can show that the offending business has infringed its rights as the proprietor or licensed user of that mark.

Copyright:

All original literary and artistic works, (which include dramatic and musical works, sound recordings, films and broadcasts) are protected by copyright under the Copyright Act 1988 without any need for registration. Computer software is similarly protected. The owner of a copyright work has the exclusive right to publish, copy, perform or broadcast it and to make an adaptation of it. Anyone, who, without the licence of the owner, seeks to make use of such a work, risks infringing the owner's rights. Such infringement will entitle the copyright owner to bring an action for damages against the infringing party, the delivery up of infringing material (or its destruction) and an injunction to restrain the infringing party from further acts of infringement.

Copyright will usually be most relevant to franchisors in providing them with protection for their operations manuals, databases, designs and drawings as well as any proprietary software they have written themselves. Ownership will normally vest in the author of the work save where it is produced by an employee in the course of their employment in which case copyright will normally belong to the employer.

Protection provided by copyright:

Since the UK adopted the European Union Harmonisation proposals the term of copyright protection for almost all categories of copyright has been extended from 50 years to 70 years from the death of the author. This period is likely to be more than adequate for any franchisor.

Whilst a copyright owner does not need to make any application to register his rights in a particular work, it is important to place a suitably worded copyright notice on printed works and to use the designation © (or the word "copyright") before the date and the author's name in order to ensure that protection is obtained in all countries that are parties to the Universal Copyright Convention. Importantly such designation demonstrates to the world the author's rights in

Placing an appropriate copyright notice at the beginning of the manual will identify the franchisor's rights in it

the work concerned. The most obvious example of this is a franchisor's operations manual which contains details of the way in which its business system operates. Placing an appropriate copyright notice at the beginning of the manual will identify the franchisor's rights in it and assist in protecting against wrongful misuse or copying of its contents by unauthorised third parties.

The other step that can be taken to protect a franchisor's intellectual property rights in its business know-how, details of which are recorded in the operations manual, is to clearly identify by means of appropriate notice at the beginning of the manual that such information is confidential. An appropriate confidentiality notice will have the effect of alerting any party into whose hands the operations manual may fall that the information is confidential and belongs to the franchisor.

Registered and Unregistered Designs:

Certain designs (particularly those of a technical nature) may be protected by registration in much the same way as a trade mark may be registered. A proprietor may have the benefit of copyright protection for such designs, but registration avoids the need for proving ownership of proprietor's rights in them and makes the licensing of such designs for use by third parties that much easier.

Functional designs are protected by an unregistered design right included within the Copyright Designs and Patents Act 1988 and by an EU Community Unregistered Design Right. The UK Act gives 10 years protection from the time any article made to the design is first marketed for sale. The EU protection is limited to 3 years. Registration in the UK and/or the EU however will give 25 years protection. A design can be protected in either or both the UK or the EU but EU registration is simple, quick and affords wider protection without detailed examination which will only occur if a design is subsequently challenged.

If franchisors have designs that form an integral part of their business or are important in relation to its products or services then careful consideration should be given at an early stage as to how best to secure protection for such designs in a way that best suits the business needs of the franchisor and any licensing to franchisees of the use of such designs.

Patents:

A franchised business may have invented, or have the rights to, a particular product or process which is sufficiently original that it may be protected by the securing of a patent. The use of that patent may then be licensed to franchisees as part of the business system. Examples of this might be a process or product for cleaning carpets or upholstery or the equipment attached to vehicles designed to pick up and clean wheelie bins, or a product or process for treating minor scratches on motor vehicles. The securing of a patent can be a time-consuming and expensive exercise. It requires careful consideration since if the resources to police the patent are not available and the patent owner does not have the financial strength firstly to secure wide protection and then to enforce it then it may be

> *The securing of a patent can be a time-consuming and expensive exercise*

better to simply rely on maintaining strict confidentiality and secrecy as to the details of the process and secure leadership in the market under a strong and widely recognised brand and thus inhibit imitators by that means.

The important point to appreciate in relation to any process or invention developed by a franchisor or its franchisees in the course of the business, and which it may wish to be the subject of a patent application, is that such protection will not be available if information relating to the process or invention is already in the public domain. Strict confidentiality should therefore be maintained until the patent application is filed.

As with all intellectual property protection (but particularly so in respect of patents) it is vital for franchisors to take professional advice at an early stage so as to both understand the options available to them and decide upon the best tactical steps to take bearing in mind their particular requirements and resources, the market in which they are trading and their aims and objectives for the business. It is very much less expensive to plan early and take the right route than to embark upon a particular strategy without proper advice and then later have to unravel it.

Domain Names:

These form an increasingly important part of the intellectual property rights of any business and, in particular, those of any business proposing to franchise. With the internet now the major marketing tool for most businesses it is vital that franchisors are able to easily direct customers to a professionally designed website for the business from which they can identify the range of products and services provided by that franchisor and its network of franchisees. Holding a domain name (or range of domain names) which clearly identify the website address of the business and that are consistent with the brand, trade name and trade marks used in the business is critical.

The franchisor will also want to ensure that its franchisees use domain names that are consistent with its brand and over which it retains ownership and control in the same way as it does over its other intellectual property rights. This control will normally be built into the obligations set out in the franchise agreement.

Whilst domain names may incorporate a trade mark they are treated differently as regards registration and, of course, domain names are accessible from anywhere in the world via the internet. Franchisors therefore need to consider carefully what domain names they need to secure not simply for their use and for use by their franchisees but also to prevent third parties obtaining them and using them to cause confusion among their customers and (potentially) damage to their business.

The domain name registries have now developed procedures for dealing with disputes arising from cyber-squatters who deliberately register domain names in bad faith with the sole intention of either extracting large sums for their transfer to the party entitled to use the trading names or trade marks which they include (or with which they are confusingly similar) or to use them to compete with or otherwise disrupt the business. There are remedies available to wrest such domain names away from such parties but franchisors, once again, need to have a clear strategy from the outset to try to minimise any problems arising for them from the use by others of such names.

The Internet and E-Commerce:

For almost every franchised business the internet will now form an integral part of the marketing strategy for itself and its franchisees both in terms of promoting goods and services and in promoting the franchise opportunity. It is clearly vital, therefore, that the website for the business is well designed as being the "cyber shop-window" for the franchise offering, for the core business itself and for the business of each franchisee. A franchisor needs to give careful consideration to both the elements of visual design for the website and its content and to the framework of the site –its architecture and the terms and conditions applicable to those using it. It also needs to decide how each franchised outlet is to be promoted on that site.

A sensible franchisor will try to ensure that its website is so well designed and effective in achieving its objectives in driving customers to its franchisees that the franchisees themselves do not have any incentive to consider setting up their own websites to promote their individual outlets. This process of website promotional activity can be controlled through appropriate provisions in the franchise agreement, not least because the franchisor will want to ensure that the design and content of any site promoting its goods and/or services are consistent with its brand image and other marketing material.

If a franchisor is to engage in e-commerce via its internet website then it will need to identify very clearly to its franchisees what benefits (if any) they will receive from e-commerce derived from customers located within any exclusive territories granted to them. Once again, this is an issue that requires careful consideration at an early stage in setting up the franchise and the particular solution will need to be tailored to the business concerned. Procedures will need to be devised that are transparent, easy to operate and fair to all parties.

Each franchisor's website will need to have well drafted terms and conditions of use to protect it and its franchisees from any problems arising from customers accessing the site. The website will also need an appropriate privacy policy designed to give them the fullest possible protection. The legal structure of the site will need to link to any e-commerce arrangements and be consistent with the terms of the franchise agreement.

The design and content of the website, as well as its overall look, are important intellectual property of the franchisor protected by copyright and the appropriate notices in that regard should be displayed on it.

Customers Data and Data Protection Act Compliance:

One of the most valuable assets of any business is likely to be its customer database. Franchised businesses are no exception. Indeed, a franchisor will need to give very careful consideration to both customer data ownership and access to and the use of such data by those within its franchised network. The way in which these issues are treated will depend to a great extent on the nature of the business itself. Some franchisors seek to maintain ownership of, and full control over, all customer data, but more usually the customer data of a franchisee will be owned by that franchisee and form a key asset of its business. The franchisor will, however, wish to ensure that it has access to such data both for itself and, frequently, for its

One of the most valuable assets of any business is likely to be its customer database

other franchisees. This is important if the franchisor or another franchisee is to ever service such customers. In addition, the franchisor will wish to monitor the performance of the franchised business and access to customer data may well be vital for that purpose.

Depending upon the type of business and the customer data which is collected, it is likely that almost all franchisors and most franchisees will need to be "notified" under the Data Protection Act 1998. This involves the registration of relevant information with the Information Commissioner's Office ("ICO") and requires each franchisee to appoint a Data Controller (being the person who controls the use of personal data within the organisation) and to inform the ICO as to the purposes for which the business processes personal data.

A franchisor's notification does not cover its franchisees, each of whom will need to be notified separately. Franchisors should therefore prescribe a notification procedure to be followed and implemented by each of their franchisees prior to the commencement of their franchised business. An experienced franchise lawyer will be able to advise on this issue and have procedures for attending to this and ensuring that each franchisee is notified concurrently with executing the franchise agreement. It is a process that franchisors simply cannot afford to ignore.

All customer and employee information must be processed in accordance with the seven data protection principles. These are designed to ensure fair and lawful processing of personal data relevant to customers and employees. Prior to the collection of such data the business must make certain details available by way of a prominently displayed data protection notice. In addition customers and employees must be informed of their right to access certain information at any time upon request.

Prior to outsourcing certain aspects of the business to third party "data processors", such as waste managers or payroll companies etc, each franchisee in its capacity as a business owner must require any such data processor to sign a data processor contract. This ensures their compliance with data protection legislation and is an issue that should be carefully reviewed when the franchise agreement is being drafted and the scope of the business model is clear.

Business owners must generally obtain the customer's prior consent and observe strict procedural requirements before directly marketing their products and services to customers. Franchisors should therefore devise procedures for their franchisees to follow which ensure strict compliance with the provisions of data protection legislation, not least since failure to comply with the 1988 Act can lead to an unlimited fine or criminal prosecution and/or civil actions for unlimited damages. The damage to a franchised brand caused by the adverse publicity surrounding any such action should not be underestimated.

The important point for franchisors to appreciate is that customer data is an important asset of the business over which it needs to have appropriate control. Compliance with data protection legislation is critical and franchisors should therefore work with their professional advisers to devise both a comprehensive policy within their operations manual dealing with data protection compliance and procedures for ensuring that all franchisees are appropriately notified so that data within the franchise network can be used in the way in which the franchisor requires. If a franchisee is not notified and the franchisor has to terminate the franchise agreement because the franchisee is in breach of its terms the franchisor may find that it cannot secure the transfer to it of valuable customer data because the franchisee is not permitted to transfer it. That situation can be avoided if the franchisee is properly notified in a manner consistent with the franchisor's requirements for data access and use.

Conclusions:

The franchisor's intellectual property lies at the very heart of the franchise arrangement, since it is a licence of those intellectual property rights to the franchisee which underpins the whole franchise arrangement. Identifying, firstly, the scope of those rights and then taking steps to protect them (where that is possible or appropriate) is as vital for the franchisor as it is for its franchisees.

> *The franchisor's intellectual property lies at the very heart of the franchise arrangement*

SHOULD THE TERMS OF A FRANCHISE AGREEMENT BE NEGOTIABLE?

WHAT DO YOU DO IF A CHANGE IS REQUIRED TO THE STANDARD TERMS OF THE FRANCHISE AGREEMENT?

By Jonathan Chadd, Partner, Leathes Prior Solicitors

The Benefit of Uniformity:

The whole essence of a franchising arrangement is one of uniformity; i.e., from a consumer perspective the products or services delivered under the franchisor's brand are of the same quality from any franchised outlet. To ensure that this is the case each franchisee must accurately replicate the franchisor's proven business system. It is thus important that each franchisee operates under the terms of an identical agreement. To agree different commercial, or other, terms for each franchisee is to invite dissention and unrest within the network, particularly where one or more franchisees consider that other franchisees are operating under less onerous terms than they are. More seriously it risks compromising the quality of the end product or service in its delivery to customers and thus the viability of the business.

The basic principle then is that a franchise agreement is in a standard form, the terms of which are not negotiable, but which are fair to both parties and (ideally) drafted in accordance with the British Franchise Association's ("BFA's") and the European Franchise Federation ("EFF") Codes of Ethics.

Having said that, however, there will always be exceptions to the rule and the first of these is the pilot operation.

The Pilot Operation:

Pilot franchisees are usually operating what is, essentially, an unproven business model and are assisting the franchisor in gathering the data that demonstrates that the model works as a stand alone independent operation. They are also identifying improvements that can be made to it before it is offered more widely for sale to franchisees.

The pilot franchise will invariably therefore need to contain terms that differ slightly from those of the standard form franchise agreement, not least with regard to the amount of the initial fee to be paid and the duration of the agreement. The initial fee will usually be discounted to reflect the additional commercial risk that the pilot franchisee is taking on by operating the unproven pilot business. A typical pilot franchise agreement may only be for one or two years after which the pilot franchisee will invariably have the right to convert across to a full standard form franchise agreement for a full five year (or longer) term without the payment of any further fee but otherwise on the franchisor's standard terms.

> *The initial fee will usually be discounted to reflect the additional commercial risk*

Special Circumstances:

The second exception to the standard form agreement will be where the circumstances of a particular franchisee are such as require adjustment to be made to the standard terms. For example, it may be because the franchisee has prior experience in the particular business concerned and would want the restrictive covenants on termination of the agreement to be modified to reflect that. The franchisee might own premises suitable for use in the business and the standard provisions relating to premises might need to be modified to address those circumstances. A franchisee might agree to take up two (or even more) franchises and as a result of that agreement might be offered concessionary terms as to the amount of the initial fee to be paid for the second and subsequent franchises. A franchisee might have other business interests which the franchisor is happy for him to continue to maintain, subject to his devoting sufficient time and attention to the franchised business so as to ensure its success.

All of these and other, similar, issues will be best addressed, not by changing the franchise agreement itself, but by acknowledging them in a Side Letter to the franchise agreement, executed concurrently with it and expressed to form part of it. If not in a Side Letter this might equally well be affected by a Deed of Variation. In any event, the important point is that the changes to the standard form are reflected in a separate document and are thus readily identifiable against the standard. This is important because franchisors and their franchisees become very familiar with the standard form document over time and it avoids the need to go through the agreement clause by clause to identify the change to the standard which can be readily seen from the separate document (Side Letter/Deed of Variation) itself.

Another circumstance in which special terms may be agreed and recorded in a Side Letter will be where a franchisee takes up more than one franchise from the franchisor operating the business in two or more separate territories often through separate companies. His involvement in more than one franchised outlet will necessitate changes to the standard terms to reflect (for example) the fact that the franchisee may not require the initial training and may be paying a discounted initial fee. These will usually be best recorded in a Side Letter rather than within the franchise agreements themselves.

These changes are not such as to discriminate between one franchisee and another in their operation of the business model but simply reflect the particular circumstances of an individual franchisee at the time the franchise agreement is entered into. Importantly, the manner in which they are recorded allows the franchisor to maintain that all franchisees are operating under the same agreements.

Changes in the Business System:

Over time the franchisor's business system will change. Improvements will be made to it, new systems will be developed, new procedures devised and new products or services included within those authorised by the franchisor as those which may be offered by its franchisees to customers. These changes may necessitate changes to the franchise agreement itself in order to reflect what is required of the franchisee and/or the franchisor and the relationship between them and/or what is required of the franchisee in the delivery of the products or services under the franchised brand.

Changes in Legislation:

Similarly, there may be changes in legislation which impact upon particular provisions within the franchise agreement or require additional provisions to be included in it so as to ensure the franchisee's compliance with such legislation. A good recent example of this is the Bribery Act 2010 which has led to many franchisors including a provision in their franchise agreements specifically requiring franchisees to comply with that legislation. Another example is the rapidly extended use of social media and the potential damage that that can cause to a franchised network through misuse by disgruntled franchisees. All prudent franchisors will now include a provision in their agreements specifically addressing the use and/or misuse of social media by franchisees.

Prudent franchisors will now include a provision in their agreements specifically addressing the use and/or misuse of social media

These amendments require changes to be made to the agreement itself which will, in any event, evolve over time. The standard form agreement will, therefore, mutate into different versions over a period of years as new agreements are issued to new franchisees and/or existing franchisees renew their franchises through the grant of new agreements on the then standard current terms.

Renewal:

Where a franchisee is renewing his franchise by the grant to him of a successor agreement the renewal terms will differ from those of the original agreement and from those of a new agreement for a new franchisee who has not already been trained in the system and procedures of the franchisor's business and will need assistance in launching the business in a wholly new territory.

These differences will either be reflected in a renewal/successor agreement (from which the terms relevant only to a new franchisee have been removed) or (more usually) in a Side Letter to the standard form agreement which will record the circumstances of the renewal and identify the changes to the standard terms agreed between franchisor and franchisee. The result is the same – a renewal of the franchise under the standard form agreement but excluding certain of the parties' initial obligations.

Operations Manual:

For an existing franchisee the terms of the agreement will remain the same through its initial term. Any amendments to it during its term would need to be agreed between both franchisee and franchisor. The franchisor does, however, have a means of effecting changes to the business system through the operations manual. This is expressed to form part of the agreement but can be changed at any time as the franchisor determines. Thus changes in procedures and in the day to day operation of the business can be effected through simply making a change to the manual with which the franchisee is obliged to comply. The manual (and any changes to it) must, of course, be and remain consistent with the terms of the franchise agreement itself and be reasonable and proportionate but it does allow the franchisor a means of introducing changes at any time during the life of a franchise agreement and of introducing improvements to the system.

> *Changes in procedures and in the day to day operation of the business can be effected through simply making a change to the manual*

Changes to Parties to the Agreement:

The other circumstance under which a mechanism for effecting changes to the franchise agreement is required is when there is a change in one of the parties to it. This is most likely to occur where one of the principals of a franchisee company decides to retire from the business, dies, or becomes incapacitated, and wishes to be removed from his obligations as a principal and guarantor under the agreement. Whether or not it is proposed to substitute a new party in his place such a change can readily be effected by a Deed of Variation which simply records the change being made by the agreement of all parties. Like the Side Letter this document enables a franchisor to readily identify changes made to the original agreement in its standard form.

Entire Agreement Provision:

The franchise agreement will invariably contain a clause expressing it and the operations manual to constitute the entire agreement between the parties. It will expressly exclude from that agreement any other terms warranties or representations made by the franchisor or its directors or employees unless in writing and annexed to the franchise agreement and expressed to form part of it. Thus any replies given by the franchisor to enquiries raised by the franchisee will need to be so annexed to the franchise agreement in order that the franchisee may rely upon them. The Side Letter is most usually used as the mechanism used for that purpose.

Conclusion:

The whole basis of franchising is the uniformity to be found in the quality of service level delivery and product sales across the franchised network. This is achieved by franchisees diligently following the system and replicating the franchisor's business model accurately. Of course there will be minor discrepancies between different outlets and the structure needs to flexible enough to absorb those and the particular circumstances of each franchisee but the fewer differences there are between franchisees the happier and more successful they are likely to be and the fewer problems franchisors will encounter within their network.

WHAT CAN YOU DO IF A FRANCHISEE DOESN'T PERFORM OR DO WHAT THEY ARE TOLD?

By Graeme Payne, Partner, Field Fisher Waterhouse LLP

The answer to this question is twofold: firstly a franchisor should be developing a franchise model and business which minimises the opportunity and desire for a franchisee not to comply with or perform the franchisor's requirements; and secondly a well advised franchisor should have a range of options, from more informal methods through to legal action, which it feels confident and comfortable using depending on the nature of the franchisee's conduct and the relationship between the parties.

To deal with non-performing and non-compliant franchisees a well advised franchisor will have a range of options at its disposal. Such options, which are discussed towards the end of this chapter, are predominantly reactionary and used mainly in circumstances where the franchisor no longer wishes to keep the franchisee in the franchise network. In my experience "successful" franchisors, and by successful I mean those who have a stable and compliant network of franchisees consistently wishing to either renew or to expand their own franchise businesses, are those franchisors who anticipate and identify inherent risks in their business and proactively manage those risks.

For those business owners considering franchising, the value of engaging franchise specialist advisers should not be underestimated. Whilst the business owner and potential franchisor will have a far greater understanding of the business and system that it wishes to franchise, a specialist franchise adviser, particularly one with

Identify the risks in franchising the business

experience of both establishing a franchise system and of franchise disputes and litigation, will be able to help identify the risks in franchising the business.

As franchising is heavily system and process driven, it is advisable to look at parts of the franchise system and the various processes to identify where the franchisor can be exposed to risk and how to manage and reduce such risks.

Franchisee Recruitment

If the franchisor selects the wrong franchisee it is likely that the franchisee will not perform or do what they are told. If, for example, the franchisee is themselves highly entrepreneurial, there is a strong likelihood that they will not wish to follow the franchisor's business systems, processes and procedures.

In addition to assessing whether a franchisee will follow the franchisor's system and be a suitable "brand ambassador", a franchisor must also consider the franchisee's proposed trading status and finances. During recruitment a franchisor should seek appropriate evidence that a potential franchisee has sufficient working capital to cover both the initial investment in the franchise as well as the ongoing operation of the business. A franchisee with insufficient working capital is unlikely to be able to invest in marketing, growing and developing the business.

> *Seek appropriate evidence that a potential franchisee has sufficient working capital*

In addition to the franchisee's financial position, a franchisor needs to ascertain whether the franchisee is contracting as a sole trader, limited liability company, partnership or limited liability partnership. Depending on the franchisee's choice of status the franchisor needs to consider:

- Who will have access to the franchisor's confidential information and know how?
- Who will own or lease any key business assets including, for example, any business premises lease?
- Who ultimately is investing the money in and taking the money out of the franchise business?

Subject to the answers to the above and to help reduce its exposure to commercial risk, the franchisor should consider requiring:

- undertakings of non-disclosure, confidentiality and non-competition from key individuals within the franchisee's organisation; and
- personal guarantees from the main shareholder, partner or individual who owns the key assets and/or provides the finance.

Without the above protections, if the franchisee does not perform or do what they are told, for example, takes the franchisor's know-how and operates a competing business or helps a family member or friend operate a competing business, the franchisor will be exposed. If the franchisor wishes to bring an action against such individuals then, without the above agreements in place, it will not have a contractual right to do so

The Manual and the Franchise Agreement

A franchisor who wishes to proactively prevent non-performing and non-compliant franchisees needs to ensure that its franchise system and more importantly its Operations Manual and franchise agreement help it to do this.

As well as communicating the key franchise system requirements during the initial and ongoing training (see below), a franchisor must ensure that the operational requirements of the franchise system and business are clearly detailed in the Operations Manual. If the training and information disseminated both in general communication and by the Operations Manual is ambiguous or insufficient in detail, this will enable a franchisee to claim that their non-performance or non-compliance was due to poor communication and/or a lack of clarity and detail on the franchisor's behalf.

Highlighted below are just some of the processes and controls that a franchisor should consider and make sure are reflected in the franchise agreement and Operations Manual.

Training

The franchise agreement needs to provide that, where the franchisee (or the franchisee's staff) fails to meet the franchisor's standards at the end of initial training, the franchisor can either request replacement staff to be trained or terminate the franchise agreement with the franchisee without liability.

Additionally the franchise agreement and the Operations Manual should also detail what refresher training or training for new staff the franchisor will provide. In some instances the franchisor may need the right (particularly with under-performing franchisees) to compel the franchisee to make it or its staff available for further training.

Monitoring and Auditing

Both the franchise agreement and the Operations Manual need to detail the financial monitoring and reporting systems and requirements. Depending on the frequency of such reporting and/or monitoring and the extent to which the franchisor analyses this information such financial monitoring and reporting can be used to help identify non-performing or non-compliant franchisees.

Additionally the franchise agreement and Operations Manual need to expressly detail what financial and performance auditing rights the franchisor has. For example, will the franchisor undertake mystery shopper programmes, announced and unannounced visits to the franchisee's premises and what client/customer/staff feedback systems will be imposed?

148

Marketing and Business Plans

Marketing and business plans can be useful tools for both the franchisor and franchisee in terms of providing a "road map" as to marketing and business objectives and requirements to be fulfilled over a defined period.

> *Marketing and business plans can be useful tools for both the franchisor and franchisee*

Provided that the completion and updating of the business plan and any quarterly or annual business plan reviews imposed by the franchisor via the franchise agreement, are used constructively and strategically and not just "to tick a box", then, for those franchisees whose performance may be below network average or in decline, this can be a useful means to identify and help address performance issues. If, for example, a franchisee is not winning any new business and such franchisee does not have a business or marketing plan, or has not been complying with any minimum marketing spend obligations, then the business and marketing plan review undertaken by the franchisor can help raise such issues in a constructive, positive and non-antagonistic manner.

Performance Targets

Allied to business and marketing plans may be the imposition of performance targets by the franchisor on the franchisee. Such performance targets typically tend to be turnover based or a minimum product purchase requirement on the franchisee. To be of substance and to have some "bite" not only do such targets need to be set out in the franchise agreement but the agreement needs to have defined consequences in the event that the franchisee fails to achieve them. Importantly the franchisor will need to take appropriate action against those franchisees who fail to achieve such targets.

Depending on both the basis for calculation of the performance targets and the extent of the franchisee's underperformance, as a first step the franchisor should request that the franchisee attends a meeting at the franchisor's head office to discuss the franchisee's performance.

Subject to the outcome of these discussions, and assuming that both parties wish for the franchisee to remain in the network, the franchisor and the franchisee should look to agree a remedial business plan of six to twelve months in duration. One approach, approved by the British Franchise Association, is for such a business plan to oblige the franchisee to achieve, in the case of future sales targets, 70% of the average gross sales for the same period of all network franchisees operating for longer than one year.

In the event that the franchisee fails to achieve the revised performance targets, a well drafted franchise agreement should provide for a range of options including:

(i) an extension of the revised business plan and performance targets;

(ii) a reduction or increase in the size of the franchisee's territory;

(iii) withdrawal of territorial exclusivity – thereby permitting both the franchisor and other franchisees to service clients in what was a previously ring-fenced territory;

(iv) termination of the agreement and a parting of ways for the franchisor and franchisee.

Reducing The Risk of Non-Performance & Non-Compliance

The techniques and procedures outlined above are all methods that franchisors should use proactively to reduce the risk of non-performance and non-compliance. If accurately documented and logged as part of the franchisor's own franchisee CRM system they can be very powerful counter-evidence in the event that a franchisee or group of franchisees allege that the franchisor has failed to meet its support obligations.

By their nature such methods are designed to keep franchisees in the franchise network. In certain circumstances however, the nature and severity of the franchisee's non-performance or non-compliance will be such that the relationship between the franchisor and franchisee will have irreparably broken down.

What Happens When The Franchise Relationship Completely Breaks Down?

The franchisor not only has responsibilities and obligations to individual franchisees but to the whole network. If a franchisee's conduct is damaging the brand, and therefore other franchisees' businesses, it is important that the franchisor takes swift and decisive action.

A common phrase in franchising is: "if either party reaches for the franchise agreement, then it is likely that the franchise relationship is dead". Whilst the starting point for most franchise disputes is correspondence between the franchisor and the franchisee, it is true that once lawyers are involved and the parties are reviewing the terms of the franchise agreement, it is likely that one or both parties no longer wish for the franchisee to remain in the franchise network.

> *If either party reaches for the franchise agreement, then it is likely that the franchise relationship is dead*

Here the importance of a well drafted franchise agreement cannot be underestimated. At its simplest the franchise agreement needs to clearly set out:

(i)   such actions or omissions by the franchisee which constitute grounds for termination;

(ii) depending on the nature and severity of the conduct, the right for the franchisor to either terminate immediately or serve notice of its intention to terminate unless the breach of the franchise agreement is remedied to the franchisor's satisfaction within a defined period; and

(iii) the dispute resolution procedure.

Grounds For Termination

It is important that the termination provisions of the franchise agreement in particular the grounds for termination are clear and unambiguous.

If, for example, a franchisee goes bankrupt, or operates a competing business to that of the franchisor, or shares the franchisor's confidential information with third parties, then these should be defined grounds for automatic termination. Such conduct is incapable of remedy and is likely to damage both the franchisor's brand and other franchisees' businesses.

By way of a different example, if a franchisee is late in paying its monthly service fees, or late in delivering a financial report, such conduct can be remedied. Extending these examples one stage further, if a franchisee is persistently late in paying its monthly service fee and/or delays payment significantly beyond the requisite payment date, or consistently fails to deliver important business information, this will impact on the franchisor. If such conduct is replicated by other franchisees the system and processes which make the particular franchise model successful begin to break down.

The franchise agreement therefore needs to provide that where a franchisee is persistently in breach; or commits a number of separate but different breaches; or fails to remedy breaches within a certain period; or fails to remedy breaches to the franchisor's satisfaction, all constitute grounds for the franchisor to serve notice and terminate the franchise agreement.

Dispute Resolution Procedure

Where a potential dispute has arisen, or in the event that the franchisor has identified non-performance, underperformance or non-compliance by a franchisee, as a first step most franchisors arrange to have a formal meeting with the franchisee to discuss the issues. Depending on the outcome of that meeting and/or

As a first step most franchisors arrange to have a formal meeting with the franchisee to discuss the issues

any reluctance on the franchisee's behalf to meet, if the situation cannot be amicably resolved, it is likely that a franchisor, if it has not already engaged specialist franchise dispute resolution lawyers, will now do so.

Most franchise agreements typically provide for either High Court litigation or as a preliminary step a form of alternative dispute resolution ("ADR") as the dispute resolution procedure. Some franchise agreements, but only a very few, may contractually oblige the parties to settle their disputes via arbitration.

A brief description of these different options and their relative merits are set out below. First however I will explore the situation where a franchisor needs to act extremely swiftly i.e. those scenarios where a franchisee is causing significant brand damage, for example where a franchisee is competing with the franchisor or sharing the franchisor's trade secrets and confidential information with third parties.

Here time pressures dictate that remedies such as High Court litigation or mediation will be too slow in resolving the issue. It is likely that the franchisor will have tried to arrange a meeting and/or engaged lawyers to send correspondence requiring the franchisee to stop their conduct but such methods have proved unsuccessful. In this scenario the franchisor needs to consider applying for an injunction.

Injunctions

An injunction is typically an order from the court that requires a party to stop doing a specific act. For example, an injunction can be used to enforce a restrictive covenant in a franchise agreement such as an obligation on the franchisee not to compete with the franchisor. In determining whether to award an injunction a court will balance the harm caused to the franchisor by the continued franchisee's trade against the harm to the franchisee caused by the cessation of the franchisee's competing business. The court will also consider whether the likely harm to the franchisor might be compensated by money damages, in which case it will be less likely to grant an injunction.

As explained by the Court of Appeal in *ChipsAway International Ltd v Kerr*, the purpose of the restrictive covenant is essentially to preserve the franchisor's goodwill in the franchisee's former territory while it seeks a replacement franchisee. Provided the court is satisfied that the balance of convenience operates in favour of the franchisor, an injunction will be granted to restrain the former franchisee and prevent irreversible and/or unquantifiable damage to the franchisor's business.

Litigation

For scenarios where the franchisor does not need to act so swiftly, the franchise agreement usually dictates the dispute resolution procedure. Most English franchise agreements will provide that any disputes between the parties shall be resolved by High Court litigation.

> *The decision to pursue a litigation claim should not be taken lightly by franchisors*

The decision to pursue a litigation claim should not be taken lightly by franchisors and will be reserved for those scenarios where the relationship between the franchisor and franchisee has irretrievably broken down.

Litigation is likely to be an unwanted distraction to franchisors. If managed and handled correctly it can however send an important message to the rest of the franchise network and help persuade other franchisees to comply with the franchisor's requirements.

The traditional perception that litigation conjures up is one of arduous procedural rules, delay and expense. This is still true to a degree but since the Civil Procedure Rules ("CPRs") came into force, the courts now have case management obligations to manage cases efficiently, including identifying issues at an early stage and assisting the parties in settling the case.

At various stages in a dispute, the CPRs encourage and require the parties to consider ADR (see below). Litigation is typically more rigid and formal in procedure than ADR. It is also generally a slower process than ADR and disclosure obligations alongside other factors push up costs for all concerned. The issue of costs can sometimes be used tactically in a dispute situation. As discussed above, litigation is not an option for parties who want to retain an ongoing commercial relationship as the proceedings are antagonistic in nature.

ADR – Mediation

Whilst the majority of franchise agreements do not expressly provide for mediation as a dispute resolution mechanism it is the most commonly used form of ADR in franchise disputes and is an option that can be chosen by the parties even if not provided for in the franchise agreement.

Mediation is a flexible, non-binding process where an independent third party is appointed to bring the parties together to identify the issues in dispute, facilitate discussion and attempt to reach a negotiated settlement.

Mediation is a quicker and cheaper procedure than going to court

One of the main advantages of mediation is its success rate: a Centre for Effective Dispute Resolution audit in 2010 found that 75% of cases settle on the day of the mediation, with a further 14% settling soon after[1]. Mediation is a quicker and cheaper procedure than going to court, although there will still be costs involved in preparing case summaries, mediator's fees and venue costs.

Mediation is a potential solution if both franchisor and franchisee wish to preserve their business relationship: it is less adversarial than court proceedings or arbitration, and the discussions are confidential and on a without prejudice basis. Any settlement reached by mediation is not binding until both parties sign a settlement agreement reflecting the agreed terms – this can then be enforced as a matter of contract law.

Parties may however be reluctant to mediate instead of litigate. With mediation there is less disclosure of documents than with court proceedings, and parties may be worried about settling without complete knowledge of the strength of the other's case. Further mediation is sometimes seen as a stalling tactic to postpone court proceedings, and will not necessarily be cost effective in circumstances where the parties are unable to settle during mediation and are forced to undertake the additional expense of litigation.

---

[1]http://www.cedr.com/news/?347

Arbitration

Arbitration is generally thought to sit outside the ADR umbrella. In a small number of cases franchise agreements may expressly oblige the parties to arbitrate. If a party attempts to litigate in breach of an arbitration clause in a franchise agreement then the court will stop the proceedings.

One advantage of arbitration is that the parties have some flexibility in which procedures they want to follow, which can help parties to save time and costs compared with litigation.

The arbitrator is an independent individual who is jointly selected by the parties, often on the basis of their qualifications or expertise in a chosen field. This can differ from litigation: a judge allocated by the court to a case is unlikely to have as much specialist expertise as an arbitrator carefully chosen by the parties. Arbitration is private

Arbitration is private and confidential between the parties

and confidential between the parties, which saves any embarrassment from unwanted publicity. This is one of the main attractions for franchisors in adopting arbitration over litigation.

Arbitration ends when the arbitrator makes an award, which can then be enforced within the United Kingdom as a court order. One of the disadvantages of arbitration is that there are very limited grounds for appeal.

Avoiding & Managing Disputes – Conclusion

In conclusion, proactive identification of risk of non-performance and non-compliance by franchisees should be a starting point for all franchisors – both at the start of the franchise journey and as a continuing process as the franchise business and network grows and develops. Such proactive techniques can also help to defeat any claims by individual or groups of franchisees that the franchisor has failed to deliver on its support obligations.

In those scenarios where the franchisor no longer wishes for the franchisee to remain in the franchise network, or the franchisee's conduct is such that by remaining in the network it causes damage to both the brand and the network as a whole, a franchisor will need to take swift and decisive action. In such cases an injunction, mediation, arbitration or litigation are the key options that a franchisor needs to consider.

8

QUESTION 11

IF A FRANCHISEE WILL BE OPERATING FROM COMMERCIAL PREMISES WHO SHOULD TAKE THE LEASE, THE FRANCHISEE OR FRANCHISOR?

By Graeme Payne, Partner, Field Fisher Waterhouse LLP

For the purposes of this answer I have assumed that neither party will acquire the property outright i.e. own the freehold title and therefore will focus on which party has the leasehold title. There is no right or wrong or standard approach answer to this question: either the franchisor or the franchisee can take the lease. From a pure property perspective, the franchisor has three main options: (i) the franchisee takes the lease and the franchisor has no legal interest in the property; (ii) the franchisee takes the lease but the franchisor has an option to acquire the leasehold title from the franchisee; or (iii) the franchisor takes the lease of the property and then underlets to or permits occupation by the franchisee.

162

In addition to seeking advice from its property and franchise lawyers (who ideally should be under one roof), the option that an individual franchisor decides to follow will depend on a number of factors, including the franchisor's attitude to risk and control, the franchisor's growth plans, available capital resources, roll-out schedule, available and suitable members of the franchisor's staff and the franchisor's exit plans. Over and above all of these factors, a franchisor will need to ask itself: "What is the right approach for me as the franchisor?" and "What is the right approach for the franchise business?"

It is important that the franchisor's property strategy fits with the franchise strategy. A franchisor looking to grow a successful franchise business will not wish to become distracted from its main obligations to the franchise business and franchisee network if a large proportion of its time and capital is spent managing a property portfolio and all the attendant issues that accompany commercial premises and business tenants.

Conversely having a portfolio of properties in strategic locations under the franchisor's management and control may be vital to the franchise model as well as the franchisor's peace of mind. For those franchisors looking to build a successful franchise business with a third party sale, third party investment or flotation in mind, having a portfolio of freehold, or more commonly leasehold properties, can add significant value when the franchisor comes to exit.

For the purposes of this answer I have assumed a relatively simple and straightforward franchise business model: where the franchisor grants a franchisee the right to operate the franchise business from a set of premises. Whilst a number of the considerations detailed above and below apply to most franchise models and systems, I have not answered the question within the context of joint venture franchising, area/regional development franchising i.e. where franchisees tend to be multi-unit or multi-site franchisees or management franchising which is a common model adopted by a number of the larger franchised hotel chains. As stated above, for the purposes of this answer, I have focused on either the franchisor or the franchisee taking a leasehold interest i.e. the right to occupy as opposed to a freehold interest i.e. outright ownership.

Option 1: Franchisee takes the lease, franchisor has no legal interest in the property

The first option outlined above is where the franchisee takes the lease and the franchisor has no legal interest in the premises.

For franchisees, this option can be problematic if landlords of prime locations are not willing to grant leases (or preferential commercial terms) without financial backing from the franchisor.

The advantages of this option for the franchisor are that no costs will be incurred with respect to drafting and negotiating the lease documentation and the franchisor will not have any obligations in respect of the lease itself.

The principal disadvantage is that the franchisor has no control over the property. A well advised franchisor with a well drafted franchise agreement – which will need both franchise and commercial property expertise – can to some extent mitigate this lack of control through enforcing the provisions of the franchise agreement and the Operations Manual which relate to the commercial premises and the franchisee's conduct in relation to it.

> *The principal disadvantage is that the franchisor has no control over the property*

Where commercial premises are a key component and requirement of the franchise model, it is essential that the franchise agreement and the Operations Manual document a clear process from site and premises selection criteria, through fit out, to the point of opening to the public. Without these key checks and balances the franchisor runs the risk of poor quality sites and premises and inconsistency within the network as to the style and fit out which as a result will damage and devalue the franchisor's brand. It is therefore important that the franchise agreement provides the franchisor a right of veto over the site and premises, the terms of the lease which are being offered to the franchisee and the right to inspect, approve and disapprove the fit out of the premises.

In this Option 1 scenario where the franchisor has no legal interest in the property, the franchisee should be obliged via the franchise agreement to procure entry and access rights to the property for the franchisor – as from a pure property perspective the franchisor has no rights to enter into the property and therefore may not be able to inspect the running of the franchise operation.

One significant disadvantage of this option is that, in the event the franchisee fails to comply with the terms of their lease and their right to occupy the property is terminated, the franchise arrangement as a whole will be jeopardised. This will have negative consequences for both the franchisor and the franchisee.

A further consequence of the franchisor's lack of control from a property perspective is that if either party terminates the franchise agreement, the franchisor will not be able to replace the outgoing franchisee with a new franchisee in the same property. Following either termination or expiry of the franchise agreement the franchisee will therefore be able to continue to trade from the premises potentially eroding the franchisor's brand's goodwill.

With Option 1, depending on the terms of the franchise agreement, the franchisor therefore runs the risk of losing a good location and set of premises and potentially the ability to exploit the surrounding territory and customer base. This lack of control on termination therefore has the potential to damage the profitability of the operation.

It will therefore be important to ensure that the franchise agreement has appropriate post termination and post expiry restrictive covenants restricting how the franchisee can trade from the premises.

Option 2: The Franchisor has the option to purchase the lease

The second option is where the franchisee takes the lease and grants the franchisor an option to take an assignment of the lease from the franchisee in certain circumstances – i.e. an option to purchase.

Whilst some franchisors' property strategy is to have no legal interest in any of the franchisees' properties (see Option 1 above) and other franchisors always insist on taking the lease (see Option 3 below) a common strategy and one which typically evolves as the franchise network grows over a period of time – as opposed to being planned from the outset – is for the franchisor to 'cherry pick' those properties in which the franchisor has or wishes to have a legal interest. With such an approach the franchisor selects only those properties which it sees as 'premium' sites or locations over which it wishes to maintain particular control. When it comes to the franchisor's exit therefore, subject to the terms of the leases, the franchisor will be able to offer these premium sites as part of the sale transaction.

Some franchisors' property strategy is to have no legal interest in any of the franchisees' properties

One of the ways that a franchisor can engineer a scenario whereby it is able to cherry pick is by providing an option for the franchisor to obtain an assignment of the lease from the franchisee.

In addition to the flexibility that this option provides, another advantage of this approach is that in the event that the franchise agreement terminates and the franchisor exercises its option to acquire the lease, the franchisor can (provided the terms of the lease allow) replace the outgoing franchisee with a new franchisee thereby ensuring the continuity of the franchise operation from the premises. This should help to preserve any local goodwill that has been built up for the franchisor's brand at the particular location in question.

The disadvantages of this option include, from a pure property perspective, a potential devaluation of the property as a result of the franchisor's option over it. From a practical perspective and this is where due diligence will need to be undertaken in advance by both the franchisor and the franchisor's property lawyers, the ultimate owner of the property may not permit the franchisee to grant an option to the franchisor.

Should the franchisor exercise the option, in order for the lease to be assigned to the franchisor, the franchisee will, in most cases, need to obtain the landlord's consent to the assignment and it is likely that the franchisor will be required to enter into various guarantor or rent deposit covenants. The complexities of the option structure require careful thought and planning, in particular the co-ordination of the timings of the various consents, covenants, guarantees and agreements. If a franchisor needs to move quickly, the time taken to obtain both landlord's consent and for the franchisee to complete the transfer can slow matters down. Once the franchisor has a leasehold interest in the property they will have to obtain the ultimate landlord's consent to any sublettings to new franchisees (see Option 3 below) and any delays in obtaining such consent could lead to the franchise operation being suspended and therefore loss of brand goodwill if the property is empty.

Option 3: Franchisor takes a lease of the property

The third option is where the franchisor takes the lease of the property and grants an underlease to the franchisee.

The obvious and key advantage here is that the franchisor has control over the property. Whilst the franchisor will therefore have all the responsibilities and liabilities of property ownership, the franchisor will, provided the underlease is well drafted, be able to pass all site related costs and other liabilities to the franchisee. It is for example, quite usual for the underlease in this scenario to require the

> *The obvious and key advantage here is that the franchisor has control over the property*

franchisee to pay for the costs of all rates, assessments and outgoings charged to the property. Furthermore the underlease can include a service charge which will require the franchisee to reimburse to the franchisor any sums relating to the costs of maintaining or insuring the building.

The main disadvantage is that when the franchise agreement comes to an end for any reason, the franchisor will be liable for the rent and all associated costs of the property until a new franchisee can be found.

Take Specialist Property and Franchise Legal Advice

Of key importance for a franchisor adopting either the option structure (Option 2) or the ownership structure (Option 3) is to ensure that they engage lawyers who understand both the franchise model and how this fits with the property strategy. If a franchise agreement provides, for example, for a five year initial term and a five year renewal term, the franchisor will need to ensure that such renewal provisions are possible in the context of the property structure.

> *Engage lawyers who understand both the franchise model and how this fits with the property strategy*

Equally the franchisor will need to ensure – or more likely the franchisor's lawyers will need to ensure – that the franchisor will be able to get the premises back for use either by the franchisor or a new franchisee when the franchise agreement terminates. Provided that both the franchise agreement and underlease are correctly drafted and 'fit together', should the franchise agreement and or the underlease be terminated for breach by the franchisee, then the franchisor should be able to have the franchisee removed. As a separate but related consideration the franchisor's lawyers will also need to ensure that the franchisee can be removed from the property once the franchise agreement ends i.e. the franchisee must not be granted 'security of tenure'.

Avoiding Security of Tenure

Unless expressly excluded security of tenure applies automatically to any commercial lease to (broadly) allow a business tenant (i.e. the franchisee or the franchisor as the case may be) which is in occupation at the end of the lease term to require a new lease to be granted to it on substantially the same terms. In order to exclude such a right the franchisor must serve a warning notice on the franchisee and the franchisee must swear a statutory declaration in response. The underlease must also contain an endorsement in the prescribed form.

If the tenancy is structured in this manner, the franchisor may take comfort from the fact that if the term of both its lease and the underlease is the same as the franchise agreement, it will be entitled to obtain possession at the end of the term. Hence it is important to consider the length of term and any renewal of the franchise agreement in conjunction with the property lease documentation. The underlease should, however, be for a shorter period than the franchisor's lease, to ensure that the franchisor can take physical possession at the end of the term so as to be able to exercise its own right to a new lease.

In addition to the above, it is important for the underlease to contain an unconditional right for the franchisor to break the lease on a rolling basis to ensure that the underlease can be brought to an end if the franchise agreement is terminated early (for example as a result of non-performance by the franchisee). Basic forfeiture provisions alone are insufficient as the franchisee may be granted relief from forfeiture by a Court.

Conclusion

In conclusion, all three of the above options have various advantages and disadvantages for a franchisor. Having the ability to swiftly exit an underperforming franchisee from what is a good location and replace with a new franchisee is a very important control factor for a franchisor. Conversely the additional liabilities and obligations for a franchisor as both a tenant and a landlord, coupled with the additional administrative responsibilities may be an unwelcome burden. What is clear however is that both the franchise strategy and the property strategy must be thought through and fit together.

DO BANKS LEND TO BUSINESSES LOOKING TO FRANCHISE?

By Richard Holden, Head of Franchising, Lloyds TSB
Commercial

Finance is readily available from franchise specialist banks to support owners looking to develop their business through franchising. The bank will expect financial commitment from the business owner, a proven business model, successful pilot operations, use of reputable advisors, a sound business plan and a realistic growth strategy.

Commitment

Companies can quickly establish a regional or even a national presence within a few years through franchising. Achieving equivalent network growth through company funded development would be unthinkable. The capital required to open a franchised outlet is much less than opening a company owned store. This is due to using the franchisee's capital to fund this growth. Franchisees fund premises lease acquisition, new build or refurbishment costs, they recruit and train their staff and implement a local marketing strategy. This enables the franchise to expand without having to source new start up capital for each new outlet.

Business owners should only take the decision to franchise when they are fully armed with all the relevant information. Many people under-estimate the time commitment and capital they require to successfully expand their business through franchising. It's important for people to evaluate what resources are going to be required and how much it is likely to cost before weighing up whether it is the right option for them at that particular time. Businesses can fail because they look to expand too quickly when they have not got the financial or business infrastructure to cope with the growth.

> *Many people under-estimate the time commitment and capital they require to successfully expand their business*

Whilst banks will consider support to businesses developing through franchising there will be a significant shareholder capital investment required before gaining the financial backing of a bank. The business owner may also need to put up personal assets as security for the bank lending. Finance may be available to help develop the existing business model and to set up pilot operations. Help towards the costs of the professional consultancy and legal fees as well as franchisee recruitment may also be available, subject to status.

Proven business model

People who are effectively selling a pipedream to investors will not secure franchise development financing from the bank manager. Prospective franchisees are attracted to franchise opportunities because they offer access to an established business model which has been tried, tested and proven by the franchisor. Entrepreneurs should not look to franchise a business idea or concept that can't demonstrate a track record of success over a reasonable period of time, which would usually be at least one full trading cycle and preferably longer.

Entrepreneurs should not franchise a business idea that can't demonstrate a track record of success

Pilot Operations

By operating a pilot franchise, the franchisor can prove the viability of their franchise system. Pilot operations prove that the business can be operated at arm's length by someone who has received the appropriate training. The successful running of the pilot operation is essential to the preparation of the franchise package. The evidence of their success will be essential to gain the bank's commitment to support the development plans and ultimately to convince the first franchisees that they should choose the investment.

There is a concerning trend to launch franchises without appropriate pilot testing. This approach is not supported by franchise specialist banks because a franchisor should offer a proven successful business to investors. Without successful pilot operations the initial franchisees will be taking a significantly greater risk investing in franchises that follow this expansion route and are unlikely to secure bank funding.

Getting the right advice

When considering development finance for business owners embarking on the road to franchising the bank would favour those who have received expert guidance. It is crucial that owners who are franchising their business seek professional advice from reputable and experienced consultants and solicitors who really know what they are doing. The franchise specialist banks are a great source of impartial advice. The bank's franchise team can suggest advisors to speak to who are accredited to the British Franchise Association and adhere to their standards and ethics.

Franchise development is a major decision for any business owner. No one deliberately sets out down the wrong path however recent history is littered with numerous cases where people have tried to develop a franchise strategy alone or those who have fallen prey to unscrupulous advisors and regretted their costly mistake. With the right guidance owners are well placed to expand their franchise business successfully.

> *Franchise development is a major decision for any business owner*

Business planning

All business owners want to watch their company grow and succeed in the face of increasing competition, but achieving expansion is no easy feat. While external forces can shape a business and help it grow to some extent, for the best chance of long term growth businesses need to think ahead, plan to achieve set goals and be ready to adapt and take a chance when an opportunity arises. An essential feature for any franchise growth strategy is a comprehensive business plan.

> *The business plan should be punchy*

The business plan should be punchy and a common mistake is to make it too detailed. Ensure that it grabs the bank manager's interest. Presentation of the plan is important to create a positive impression and business owners should practice delivery of their plan beforehand so that they come across professionally. Let the bank manager have a copy of the business plan in advance so they can prepare for the meeting. Expect the plan to be challenged and the owner should be able to confidently answer questions about the operational and financial aspects of their plan.

It is often assumed that a business plan is needed just to secure funding. Whilst this is an important benefit of producing a business plan it can also assist with the management of the business such as monitoring the ongoing performance against the original benchmarks and identifying areas for development. The plan is a working document and should be regularly reviewed and updated as the business develops.

Meeting the bank manager

Some may have the misconception that bank managers are small-minded Captain Mainwarings who prefer not to lend money. The reality is bank managers want to finance sound business propositions.

Business owners and bank managers tend to think very differently. Entrepreneurs are traditionally calculated risk takers, whilst bank managers are often conservative. Put yourself in the bank manager's shoes; think about what they will be looking for when someone approaches them for finance to set up a new franchise opportunity.

Banks use a variety of tools to evaluate funding propositions although bank managers will usually base their lending decisions on the traditional canons of lending. They will look for the following:

- Character
- Capital
- Capability
- Purpose
- Amount
- Repayment
- Terms
- Security

Character

Ultimately banks will lend money when there is a very good chance they will be repaid so establishing whether the customer is trustworthy and their track record is an important consideration. The bank manager will look at whether the customer is making exaggerated claims that are too optimistic or adopt a more reasonable and conservative approach. The repayment of any previous borrowing will be looked at and for new customers, bank statements will be requested to assess the conduct of existing accounts.

Capital

The amount of bank finance requested should be in proportion to the customer's own stake. A significant capital contribution from the borrower demonstrates commitment to the business.

Capability

The bank manager will look at the borrower's skills and experience as well as their drive to build a successful business. It is rare that one individual has all the skills required to run a business and consideration will be made to the ability of the management team and key staff and potential weakness within the team.

Purpose

The bank manager will wish to establish that the purpose is an acceptable risk and in the customer's best interests. In their optimism to press ahead business owners can overlook potential problems and the lender can bring a degree of realism to the proposition.

Amount

The lender will consider whether the amount being asked for is appropriate and they may challenge any assumptions used.

The borrower should ideally have a contingency reserve of funds to fall back on in case the business takes longer than expected to achieve its goals.

Repayment

The repayment source of any lending needs to be established at the outset. Repayment will usually come from trading profits and this is where projections will be thoroughly tested by the bank. Historic trading figures and up to date management accounts are essential for existing businesses.

Terms

The interest rate margin and terms offered by the bank will reflect the risk involved in the lending. Proposals that include adequate security are likely to attract better interest rates from the lender than unsecured deals. The amount and complexity of the work involved will determine the level of fees.

The business owner's personal assets are often required as a secondary repayment source

Security

The business owner's personal assets are often required as a secondary repayment source for the borrowing. Banks do not lend to the security alone and the canons of lending thus far need to be passed irrespective of the available security.

Have clear objectives

It is essential that you are clear about what you want to achieve from the bank manager meeting. Many businesses fail because they don't have a clear strategy and objectives. Writing a business plan forces owners to address the details of their own business proposal and clarify exactly what they need to do to make it a reality.

Be prepared

With realistic goals and meticulous preparation business owners should be well placed to gain the confidence of the bank manager to support their franchising plans. While business finances will be at the centre of the dealings with the bank, the more the Bank Manager understands about the business, the more likely he or she will be able to meet the business owner's requirements.

Knowing what to say and how to say it helps to make people look professional and creditable. Someone who stumbles over their words and can't answer simple questions about their business plan will not impress.

Many of the entrepreneurs who present to the dragons on the popular BBC television programme 'Dragons Den' have little chance of securing the investment that they are looking for because they are not fully prepared and haven't clearly defined what they want to say. Consequently, they are unable to establish their own credibility and project confidence in their business.

Financing options

There is a range of financing options for businesses expanding through franchising. Owners can use their own capital, borrow from banks, family and friends or attract outside investors usually in return for equity in the business. Most businesses use a combination of these according to their specific needs.

Bank finance

When approaching the bank to finance the development costs or pilot operations the franchise has not yet been proven and the viability of the projections and level of personal security will be an important consideration. A company that has a track record of operating profitably over a number of years may have built up reserves to fund most of the development itself.

The bank's franchise department are best placed to support the owners development plans even if there is a good existing relationship with the local bank manager. Most bank managers do not deal with franchise cases on a regular basis, let alone dealing with owners looking to expand through franchising, so the local support can be mixed. The few banks that have franchise experts can provide invaluable assistance to potential franchisors.

Finance from friends and family

Friends or family are another finance option worthy of consideration. This can work well as often these arrangements are informal without the need to pay interest. Personal relationships can be damaged so it is important that each party in clear about the investment and repayment terms from the outset. It must be explained to the investor that this is risk capital and they may not get it back. However if things go well returns should reflect the risk taken.

Friends or family are another finance option

Equity finance

There maybe an option to raise equity finance. Venture capitalists are private investors who provide financing for established profit making companies that are looking to expand. Usually loans will be provided in return for share equity in a company. The investor may also seek a non-executive board position and attend monthly Board meetings to have a say in how the business is run. Venture capital is usually concentrated in the newer fast growing sectors of the economy, such hi-tech firms.

Equity finance for sums under £250,000 is usually provided by business angels rather than Venture capital firms. Business angels are wealthy, entrepreneurial individuals who provide capital in return for a proportion of the company equity. Typically angels want hands-on involvement in the business using their existing skills and experience to strengthen the company's trading performance. Investors can be found by approaching angel networking organisations.

Franchise growth strategy

The choice of franchisee is critical, particularly in the early stages of a franchise system. They can determine whether the franchise succeeds or fails. Decide on the skills they should have and create a profile detailing the necessary experience and qualifications.

The bank will expect the franchisor to forecast realistic franchisee recruitment targets and income projections. Upfront licence fees paid by franchisees should contribute to the franchisor's costs of developing the franchise, as well as recruiting and training the franchisee. The franchisor's profits come from the ongoing management service fees usually linked to the franchisee's turnover or a mark up on products and services provided.

Franchisees will inevitably take time to build their business and therefore income, so initially the fees payable to the franchisor are likely to be small. This income will build over time as the franchisee's business matures and more investors are recruited into the network. The franchisor must however have their training and support structure in place from day one which means a major capital outlay is required.

Franchisees need to know how to run their business and a comprehensive training programme will show them. Franchisees are far more likely to succeed with ongoing support and guidance. A franchise management team can fulfil this role, as well as selecting the franchisees in the first place. This essential support structure, which is required from the outset, is a business overhead for the franchisor which is unlikely to be covered by franchisee network income for several months. Business owners need to build this into their franchise development plans which will be closely scrutinised by the bank.

Setting the right level of initial and ongoing fees as well as realistic and achievable recruitment targets requires professional input and guidance. Often it's not due to a poor business concept or a flawed franchise model that franchise brands

---

Franchising is not a get rich quick scheme

---

don't get off the ground, but the lack of appreciation of the financial resources required to build the franchise network in the first place. Franchising is not a get rich quick scheme for business owners and those who think that it is will be franchising their business for the wrong reasons.

Summary

In conclusion there are several finance options available to business owners expanding through franchising although bank finance is undoubtedly the most common. Franchise specialist banks are well placed to support expansion and financial assistance is accessible to those who have well researched franchise plan supported by experienced and highly regarded advisors.

Adopting a franchising strategy provides an opportunity for expansion however this significant step requires painstaking research and shouldn't be taken lightly. Franchising a business successfully can't be achieved on the cheap and will require a considerable time and capital investment from the business owner.

In recent times there has been a noticeable increase of business owners embarking on expansion plans through franchising which have little chance of long term success. I'm encountering an increasing number of business owners who are unwilling or unable to pay for expert consultancy and legal advice to develop their franchise plans, but continue to press ahead regardless. It is simply unrealistic for anyone to think that they can successfully franchise a business without a sufficient budget and the right advice.

Without expert assistance, these new franchise opportunities are far less likely to secure the backing of a bank to support their prospective franchisees' development plans. Under-capitalised business owners who launch a franchise opportunity are putting at risk both their own and their franchisees' businesses.

The key piece of advice I could give everyone looking to secure the backing of their bank is to use the services of franchise professionals who are affiliate members of the British Franchise Association. Accredited consultants and solicitors have had to demonstrate their knowledge and experience and follow a strict code of practice. It is essential that novice franchisors receive the support and guidance of experts.

HOW DOES THE FRANCHISEE GO ABOUT GETTING FINANCE?

By Richard Holden, Head of Franchising, Lloyds TSB Commercial

Obtaining the backing of a bank that understands franchising is not as hard as you may think. Banks are open for business and they want to lend money to sound propositions. A franchise business should already have been tried and tested and when we add in the initial training and ongoing support from the franchisor it is easy to understand why some banks offer preferential terms to prospective franchisees.

Raising the required funds to finance a franchise investment does not need to be a daunting process. When a franchisee is looking to finance their investment it is best to approach a franchise specialist bank. The bank's franchise departments regularly evaluate franchises and monitor the ongoing performance of existing franchisees.

Level of finance

With any business opportunity there are risks although well established franchises generally have much higher success rates than stand alone start-ups therefore some banks are willing to consider lending a higher proportion of the total set up costs of a franchise than they would do for a new independent start-up.

> *With any business opportunity there are risks*

The level of finance available from a bank will depend upon the strength of the franchise system as well as the franchisee's business plan. Typically franchise specialist banks will lend up to seventy per cent of the total investment, subject to status and a review of a business plan. For less established franchise opportunities the financial support from a bank maybe closer to fifty per cent.

The importance of a good business plan

There is truth in the old saying *'If you fail to plan, you plan to fail'* especially when starting a new business. Those who understand the benefits of business planning are more likely to be successful than those who react to day to day operational issues and are constantly fire-fighting

> *'If you fail to plan, you plan to fail'*

problems. But planning a business is not a simple matter of scribbling down a few ideas. If a franchisee is going to make their plan work, a much more thorough approach must be adopted.

The value of a good business plan can not be overstated. The initial objective of the document is to help raise finance for the business however it will also help owners understand what they wish to achieve from the business and is an essential document to review the performance against the original projections alerting the owner to anything that is not going according to plan.

Business plan template

Banks will require a business plan to set up a bank account and consider financial support for a business. Any lender will want the prospective franchisee to demonstrate that they understand their chosen market and that they will be able to meet the financial commitment they are taking on. Most banks will be able to provide a business plan template detailing what information should be included in the document. A good business plan should cover the following areas:

- Executive Summary
- Personal details (Contact details, Age, Martial status, Dependants)

- Franchisee's experience, skills and attributes
- Objectives / Mission Statement
- Overview of the franchise
- Local market (Research, Location, Customers, Competitors)
- Business operation (Premises, IT, Vehicles, Equipment)
- Key Personnel / Management team
- Marketing strategy
- Borrowing requirements
- Capital stake and Security
- Personal Assets, Liabilities, Income and Expenditure statement
- Financial Projections (Cashflow and Profit & Loss forecasts)
- Financial Assumptions
- 3 years Financial Accounts (Existing businesses only)
- SWOT Analysis (Strengths, Weaknesses, Opportunities, Threats)
- Exit strategy

It is important to remember that it is the franchisee's responsibility to write the business plan and to present it to the bank. Most good franchisors will support their franchisees in developing an effective business plan.

Franchisors need to provide business planning support

Franchisors can provide assistance to new franchisees investing in their brand to access the finance that is available from banks. Many business plans presented to the bank simply don't shape up and they are either rejected outright or the bank manager asks for additional information to consider the proposition. Some legal advisors suggest that franchisors should not get too closely involved in the business planning process due to the possibility of leaving themselves open to a future misrepresentation claim. The truth is that franchisees need a degree of support from the franchisor to understand key financial information and assumptions that they will use to produce their financial projections and business plan narrative.

Most franchisors will provide prospective franchisees with illustrations of possible trading performance, based upon the pilot operation or existing franchisees performance, however it is up to the investor to dig deeper. They must research their local market when compiling their own projections and it is always prudent to get the franchisor to check them over before they present them to the bank. It's important for franchisors to ensure that the figures they provide franchisees are based upon recent performance. Figures produced a couple of years ago before the recession may bear little resemblance to what franchisees are likely to achieve now.

But their support shouldn't stop there! Franchisees should not be left to contact the local bank manager direct. The franchisor can facilitate an introduction to the franchise specialist banks through their franchise departments which is an important first step. Around three quarters of new franchisees come from an employed background so it is likely that they will be presenting a business plan to a bank manager for the first time. It is essential that the franchisor helps them prepare for that meeting.

First impressions count

Individuals should ensure their choice of clothing is appropriate to their industry. They should dress in the way they would if they were meeting a client. For people who aren't comfortable in a suit and tie then don't wear one, although smart appearance is advisable.

Don't ramble on and ensure answers are relevant and concise. A bank manager will expect any business owner to be self-assured when communicating their well researched plan and talk with passion about the potential of the franchise.

A bank manager will expect a business owner to be self-assured and talk with passion about the potential of the franchise

Bank loans

Commercial loans are available to businesses, subject to status. They can be used for a variety of purposes including the purchase of business assets and the set up of a franchise. All the main high street banks operate in the business loan market although it is advisable to seek the support of a bank that understands franchising. The business will borrow money and repay the loan over an agreed term. In the case of a loan for a franchise, the term will not usually exceed the length of the franchise licence. Loans can be available either at a fixed or variable interest rate. In some cases capital repayment holidays can be negotiated with the lender when setting up the loan. An arrangement fee is payable on setting up the loan.

Overdrafts

Overdrafts are generally meant to cover short term financing requirements. They are available for financing the day to day working capital requirements and businesses only pay interest when they use the facility. Overdraft facilities are usually provided for up to 12 months and the renewal is negotiated with the bank manager. Overdrafts attract an arrangement fee at the outset and at each facility renewal.

Security

When a bank provides finance to a limited company it will require the directors to sign a personal guarantee. Personal assets, such as a residential property, may also be required by the bank to cover the agreed finance. Any property used as security may be repossessed if the loan repayments are not kept up. There are various alternative forms of security which maybe acceptable to the lender, so it is advisable to speak with the bank manager to review individual circumstances.

Any property used as security may be repossessed if the loan repayments are not kept up

Enterprise Finance Guarantee scheme

Don't be put off if a prospective franchisee hasn't got any security to offer the bank. The Government backed Enterprise Finance Guarantee Scheme maybe available for those who have a strong business proposal, but who lack security that the banks usually require. Speak to the bank's Franchise Unit to discuss whether the franchisee will qualify for finance under this scheme. There is a premium which is payable by the borrower to the Government in respect of the guarantee they provide the bank for the loan, which usually makes this scheme more expensive than a fully secured bank loan.

Asset finance

Asset Finance and commercial leasing may be alternatives finance sources for the acquisition of business assets such as IT equipment and vehicles. Banks and finance companies can fund a diverse range of assets, for all types of business. This type of finance is secured against the asset itself therefore it offers the advantage of reducing the requirement for bank finance, which may need to be secured against the shareholder's personal assets.

Debtor finance

Cashflow can often be a problem for small and growing businesses. Debtor finance is a means of optimising business cashflow. Through a range of factoring and invoice discounting services banks can assist businesses that issue invoices to other businesses. Invoices can be overlooked as a flexible 'asset' within a business. As such, rather than have money tied up in invoices that are awaiting payment, the business can receive an initial payment upfront and the remainder when the customer pays the invoice to the debtor finance provider – less a service fee.

Ten tips for franchisees raising finance

- Shop around for the bank that best meets their requirements. Their existing bankers may not necessarily be the most suitable business bank.

- Contact the bank's Franchise Unit to arrange an introduction to an experienced franchise business manager based locally to them.
- The presentation of the business plan is important – Practice delivery beforehand.
- Be well prepared for the bank manager meeting to demonstrate that they have a good understanding of the business opportunity and their financial requirements.
- The financial projections should be realistic and achievable.
- Financial considerations are important but don't decide the lender on price alone.
- Consider a capital repayment holiday at the start of the loan if business is going to take time to build.
- Consider alternative finance options such as asset or debtor finance.
- Have a reserve of funds to fall back on in case the business takes longer than anticipated to get established.
- The business plan is a working document and should be referred to regularly to benchmark where the business is against the original projections. Update the business plan in case additional bank funding is required.

Lending decision

The bank manager may take a few days to review the plan and financial requirements. They may need to obtain sanction for the requested funds from the bank's Credit Department. Once the lending has been sanctioned the bank manager should set out in writing the terms of the agreed finance including the costs. If the franchisee wishes to proceed then confirm their acceptance of the bank's terms and the bank manager can prepare the documentation and security arrangements.

It is likely to take several weeks to complete the security requirements. The franchisee should work closely with their bank manager to ensure that there are no delays in releasing the funds and so that the franchisee pays their licence fee in advance of attending the initial training course. It is advisable for the franchisor to overview progress to the drawdown of the funds and be prepared to step in to assist the process when necessary.

Building the relationship

Many business owners rely on the services provided by banks, so it can be very important to develop a strong relationship. Communicate regularly with the bank manager to keep them informed about developments in the business. Individuals will demonstrate that they have their finger on the pulse if they provide regular updates. This will breed confidence in their ability to manage the ups and downs of the business lifecycle.

Franchisors should keep the bank's franchise team updated

Developing strong relationships with suppliers is a key element to building any successful business. The bank's franchise department should be viewed as an important supplier to any franchise business. Franchise brands are constantly developing so it is important to provide the bank an update every six months.

Franchisors who regularly update the bank's franchise department about developments in their network are helping their franchisees gain the financial assistance they need from the bank. Ultimately, a lack of recent information about the franchise could mean that franchisees don't secure the best possible deal.

Summary

It's not hard to see why franchising is an attractive route into self employment. Experts generally regard franchising as a less risky option and statistics confirm that commercial failure rates amongst franchised businesses are much lower than independent start ups. Some banks regard franchising as a key market and financial assistance is available to support potential investors get their franchise started.

Experts generally regard franchising as a less risky option

I frequently see people approach the bank for finance but clearly they have not done their homework. They don't have a viable business plan and they are unable to answer the most basic questions about the business in a convincing manner. Don't let prospective franchisees fall into this trap – a little preparation goes a long way.

The business plan should demonstrate to the reader that the owner understands the business opportunity and the local market for the product or service. Franchisors should support their franchisees in developing their plan and preparing for meeting the bank manager to ensure that they are well placed to secure the bank funding they require.

WHAT ARE THE BEST WAYS OF ADVERTISING A FRANCHISE?

By Clive Sawyer, Managing Director, Business Options

As with any type of marketing, to be successful it is essential that you are clear about who you want to see or hear your marketing message. This is the same for franchise recruitment marketing. The first step must be to create a detailed franchisee profile. Only once this profile has been created is it possible to develop an effective recruitment marketing strategy which targets those individuals of the franchise being offered.

I have specifically talked about marketing a franchise opportunity rather than advertising as advertising is only one type of marketing. Marketing is a highly complex topic and there have been thousands of books written on the subject. The Chartered Institute of marketing have defined marketing as "The management process responsible for identifying, anticipating and satisfying customer requirements profitably." There are many different marketing processes that can be used to let prospective franchisees know about a franchise. As this is a book containing questions and answers specifically relating to franchising and not marketing I will risk the wrath of professional marketers by focusing on just five different ways that franchisors need to consider when developing their franchisee recruitment marketing plan:

- Online
- Off the page
- Exhibitions, Shows & Events
- Press Releases
- Word of Mouth

Online:

Online media encompasses both marketing on the internet as well as marketing using online social media. Looking at traditional internet marketing first, it is important to realize that this can take many forms. The first step for franchisors when considering online marketing should be setting up a page on their own website, providing details about their franchise offering. Using a business' own website is a free medium and is something most prospective franchisees would expect to find. I have had some

Some franchisors who are worried about promoting their franchise on their own website

franchisors who are worried about promoting their franchise on their own website for fear of how their customers may perceive them. I struggle to see the logic with this. If a business is going to franchise then it is likely that their customers will find out about it. Therefore it is far better to embrace the fact that they are franchising rather than trying to hide the fact. It is also important to consider the impression this will send prospective franchisees if a business doesn't seem to fully support the fact that it is franchising.

One of the key elements that makes a business a franchise is that the customer enters into a contract with the franchisee and not the franchisor. In order that customers are clear who they are contracting with, it is a legal requirement for franchisees to state on their letterhead, emails and other legal documents that they are a business operated under franchise and independently owned. Therefore customers are going to find out that the company is operating a franchise. The company should either embrace franchising and therefore have no worries about promoting it on their website or not franchise at all.

Once a business has publicised their franchise offering on their own website they can then consider other websites to be represented on. These can be split into two categories: franchise websites and non franchise websites.

There are many franchise website directories that franchisors can market their franchise on. The beauty of and the trouble with the internet is that anyone can register a domain name and anyone can create a website. Therefore just because there is a website that says they advertise franchises for sale doesn't necessarily mean that they will be any

Understand the physiology of internet users

good or suitable for every franchisor. When considering which franchise website to advertise on it is important to understand the physiology of internet users. Typically when people key in a search on the internet they will scroll down no more than three pages, many will only look on the first page of their search results. Therefore, do some simple tests first. Type in common words that describe your franchise and see which franchise website directories appear on the first page. As it is important to be seen by as many people as possible, then paying to be on the most popular websites is probably a good starting point. Also consider what type of qualification process the site undertakes. Franchisors need to determine whether they whether they want to process the details of everyone who registers an interest in their franchise or only those that meet their franchisee criteria. The more qualified approach will reduce the number of enquiries but does improve their quality.

When undertaking online franchise marketing, it is important to consider non franchise websites. This may appear a strange thing to say however if a business has created their franchisee profile and is looking for people with specific skills, experience or background then some industry websites may be worth advertising on. As an example, if a lawn care franchise only wants people that have been green keepers at golf clubs as their franchisees, then it does not make sense advertising on franchise websites as very few green keepers will likely view them. However it would make sense advertising a franchise on "Pitchcare", the website for green keepers! Equally if a business is looking for experienced salespeople; they could advertise their franchise on one of the websites that specifically targets sales professionals. Non franchise websites work equally well for part-time franchises and full-time franchises. If a part-time

Non franchise media is not right for every franchise

franchise is targeting mothers with young children as their franchisees, advertising on non franchise websites such as "mother and baby" or "working mums" may be appropriate. The benefit with advertising on non franchise websites is that there will be much less competition from other franchises compared with advertising on a specialist franchise website. Non franchise media however is not right for every franchise. If the franchisee profile is very generic and virtually anyone could be suitable as a franchisee it would be best to advertise on a franchise specific website as most people who view these franchise websites are actually interested in becoming a franchisee which is not the case with non franchise media.

Whichever online media approach a business adopts, if it is to be successful the first step has to be creating a detailed franchisee profile. Only then can there be a realistic chance of targeting the right people using the most appropriate media.

Off the Page:

When people take about "off the page" media, they are referring in the main to magazines and newspaper advertising. There are a number of magazines dedicated to franchising as well as national and local newspapers that have regular franchise sections that advertise franchises. Historically off the page advertising was the most popular media for marketing franchise opportunities, however in the last two years off the page advertising has been over taken by online media as the most popular medium. The two main reasons why franchisors are moving away from off the page advertising is the cost and the lifespan of the advert. Off the page advertising, on the whole, costs far more than most other forms of marketing. In addition, depending on the type of off the page media used, an advert may only be current for a month, in the case of most franchise magazines, or a week for most national newspapers.

This means that there is only a short time for prospective franchisees to see the advert.

On a positive note however, people that do buy a franchise magazine are normally actively looking for a franchise and therefore a well constructed franchise advert can be very effective. The national and regional newspapers that have a regular franchise section play a role in making people aware about franchising as an option to owning a business. It is important for franchisors considering advertising using national and regional newspapers to look at the demographics of the readership and compare this against the franchise profile they have created. Certain newspapers will be more appropriate to advertise in for certain franchises than for others. National newspapers also focus on different sectors each week, so choosing the most appropriate week to advertise is very important.

People that buy a franchise magazine are normally actively looking for a franchise

Exhibitions, Shows and Events:

The UK has a long history of regional and national franchise exhibitions and shows. Depending on which franchise exhibition or show a franchisor wishes to exhibit at, there will be different entry requirements. A number of the longest running franchise exhibitions require exhibitors to be either members of the British Franchise Association or where not members, they must have been accredited by the British Franchise Association to exhibition status. Some of the newer franchise exhibitions and shows have less stringent exhibitor entry requirements with the exhibition organisers undertaking their own internal review and assessment of each franchisor that applies to exhibit. British Franchise Association accreditation is of course a valuable indicator as to the professionalism of a franchise however there are many very good franchises that are not accredited by the British Franchise Association, and therefore the exhibitions and shows not regulated by the British Franchise Association have a very valuable role to play in promoting and marketing franchises.

Franchise exhibitions and shows run regularly throughout the year. The largest franchise exhibitions are normally held in February/March and also in September/October. The smaller franchise exhibitions and shows are then interspersed throughout the remainder of the year.

These franchise exhibitions and shows prove popular with people looking to become franchisees as it gives them an

Franchise exhibitions and shows run regularly throughout the year

opportunity to see a range of franchises on display at one time, as well as providing them with the opportunity to talk to the franchisors. The Franchise exhibitions and shows usually have a number of professional franchise service providers also exhibiting. These range from the high street banks that have dedicated franchise departments, to franchise consultants, accountants, solicitors and other franchise media providers. At most franchise shows and exhibitions, seminars are held covering a range of topics for both prospective franchisees and businesses looking to expand through franchising.

Not surprisingly there is a large difference between the cost of exhibiting at a national franchise exhibition compared to a local franchise show. There is also a large difference in the number of people who attend the national franchise exhibitions compared to the local franchise shows. However, local franchise shows should not be discounted as they have the advantage that most visitors by their nature will be local. Therefore if a franchisor is looking to recruit a franchisee in a specific part of the country where local franchise shows are run, can be a very good targeted approach to franchise recruitment.

The national franchise exhibitions will attract visitors from all over the UK as well as international visitors looking for UK franchise opportunities that would be interested in expanding their franchise operation overseas.

In addition to the specific franchise exhibitions and shows, there are a number of business events that include a franchise section. These range from chamber of commerce events to local business networking events as well as community backed events. As with the local franchise shows local events can be a good way to market a franchise opportunity to a local audience.

Press Releases:

Press releases are often a form of marketing that is overlooked by the majority of franchisors. Most media providers, whether they are magazine editors, franchise websites, or local and national papers, are all looking for interesting stories. The launch of a new franchise can often be of interest to media providers so it is important that when launching a franchise that press releases are sent to all media editors.

The downside with press releases is that there is no guarantee that it will be published. Media providers receive many more press releases than they have space to publish. This lack of space can also be exacerbated at certain times of the year, such as the lead up to franchise exhibition and shows, as well being affected by other news worthy items. Therefore it is important to time when press releases are sent and if they are

It is important to time when press releases are sent

not published straight away to persist with submitting information to media providers.

It is important to also know that there is a specific format that media providers require press releases to be submitted. The layout, format and information provided is very important if a business if going to stand a chance of getting their press release published. If a business is not experienced in writing press releases, they would be well advised to seek the services of a professional press release writer.

Press releases are also not just for the launches of a franchise. Anything of news worthy interest should be sent to media providers. This could include a franchisee winning an award, or the fifth, tenth, twenty fifth or fiftieth franchise starting. The press release could be about a charity event being held or attended by a franchisee or it may be about the appointment of new member of the franchisors staff. The underlining rule with regards press releases is to send regular news worthy press releases that are well written and follow the format expected by the media providers.

When considering who to send press releases to consider both online and off the page media providers. Also send them to both franchise and non franchise media providers. The press releases should help create awareness of the franchisors brand as well as the specific franchise opportunity. It should also help build confidence in the franchise as a good and successful franchise to become part of. Finally it can also help local franchisees by raising the awareness them in their local community which in turn can help generate new business.

Word of Mouth:

Franchisors should not forget to tell people about their franchise. Franchisors and franchisees are likely to be in contact with many people in the daily course of their business. Despite all the money spent on marketing franchises, there will inevitably be people that still don't know that a franchise opportunity exists. Therefore it is important to take every opportunity to tell people about it. This word of mouth can be at formal networking events and equally when speaking to local suppliers.

Also do not forget customers and suppliers as they can also spread the word about a franchise opportunity and they will know other people that the franchisor may not know. A good way of incentivising franchisees, customers and suppliers to spread the news about a franchise opportunity is to operate a franchise referral scheme. This works on the basis that if someone tells someone else about a franchise opportunity and they go on to become a franchisee, the franchisor pays the person who original promoted the franchise a finders fee. This has the advantage that the franchisor only pays a finders fee if the person becomes a franchisee. In most cases the person who becomes a franchisee may never have known about the franchise without being told by the referrer. Even when the franchisee did know about the franchise opportunity, the additional mention of it by a referrer may be the final thing that gets them make contact with the franchisor.

There are two golden rules when running a franchise referrers scheme:

1. Make sure the financial reward is big enough. If a franchisor only offers a small reward most people will not put themselves out to spread the word as it isn't worth their effort.

2. Make sure the referrer is paid if a franchisee signs up. This may sound obvious but I know of many occasions where franchisors operate referrers scheme and do not pay the finders fee. The franchisor tries to get out of paying either by trying to say that the franchisee had already made contact with the franchisor first or they just hope the referrer will forget. Nothing is likely to stop future referrals more than a franchisor that doesn't pay up! It can also have a devastating affect by giving the franchisor a bad name, damaging the franchisors brand.

Other marketing mediums:

I have only covered a few of the main marketing mediums that can be used to market a franchise opportunity. There are of course many other ways that I have not mentioned such as: direct mail campaign, in store posters and shop window advertisements, in street signage such as bill boards, telephone kiosks, train station signs, specific sector media such as armed forces media, ethnic minority media, gay media and media targeting the over 50's.

Social media is an area which is growing at an expediential rate. More and more franchisors are using social media platforms such as LinkedIn, Facebook, YouTube and Twitter to spread the word about their franchise opportunities. Unlike other marketing media, social media is creating its own rules, whereby traditional methods of marketing such as stating upfront that one has franchise opportunities are unacceptable. Social media is more about giving help and advice and in return people viewing

Franchisors are using social media platforms such as LinkedIn, Facebook, YouTube and Twitter

a business giving this advice will be seen in a positive light. Therefore a franchisor could reply to a social media posting from someone asking about what they should look for in a good franchise, by providing a helpful set of questions that a prospective franchisee should ask a franchisor. The business

216

does not need to mention that they have franchise opportunities directly but could state that as an established franchisor the questions they advise prospective franchisees to ask would be as follows. If the person finds the response of help they are likely to have a good impression of the franchisor and then go onto the franchisors website. When they go onto the franchisor websites they will already have confidence in the franchisor, which is one of the key objectives of a good franchise recruitment strategy. I am sure that by the time you read this book, there will be new social media platforms and sites as well as new protocols for their use. The important thing to remember is that if the type of person who fits a franchisee profile is someone who uses social media then choosing not to use social media to market the franchise is a massive lost opportunity.

Franchise Recruitment Plan:

When developing any strategy whether it is how to recruit franchisees or how to launch a new product or service, it is important to formalise it by writing it down. In relation to franchisee recruitment marketing, once a business has created a clear franchisee profile and identified the various media that that a person who fits the franchisee profile will see or hear, it is essential to formalize it be creating a franchise recruitment plan.

The franchise recruitment plan is a twelve month plan showing what media will be used and when to market the franchise opportunity. This is also when budgets come into play. There will be lots of media that could be used to market a franchise which may be prohibitively too expensive. I am sure most franchisors would love to be able to run a TV franchise recruitment campaign however practically it would be too expensive. What is important is to have sufficient budget allocated to market the franchise opportunity properly. I have seen many franchisors that have spent money creating their Franchise Development Model and have invested heavily on their Infrastructure Development only to be left very little money to let people know that they are offering a franchise opportunity. This is no different to normal sales, if a company does not let their prospective customers know that they have something for sale then very few people will ever buy. It is critical that before starting down the road of franchising, that a business has a clear idea of how much franchising is going to cost, including the marketing of the franchise opportunity, and budget accordingly. If a business does not have access to the necessary funds then they would be best advised not to start the franchising process and put franchising on hold until they do have the funds.

Have sufficient budget allocated to market the franchise opportunity properly

When developing any franchise recruitment plan always refer back to the franchisee profile. If a business knows the type of person they are looking for, the media used to market the franchise opportunity should be media that the franchisee profile person will see or hear.

Evaluation:

Evaluating the success of each marketing activity undertaken is an area that is often overlooked. Despite having developed a clear franchise profiling and optimised the type, frequency and timing of the franchise recruitment marketing activities, there will be some marketing activities that prove less successful than others. It is important therefore that systems and processes are put in place to monitor the effectiveness of each marketing activity that is undertaken.

A simple and free way of monitoring which activities are producing the best results is to ask every person that enquires about a franchise where they heard about it from. Some enquiries will be obvious such as they filled out a form on the franchisors stand at a franchise exhibition. Others may be leads that come direct from a franchise website. However there may be someone enquiries are received direct by the franchisor via telephone or email. It is in these cases that it is important to ask them where they heard about the franchise. This will allow the franchisor to evaluate the success of all their marketing activities and stop marketing in those media which are not producing results and redirect the expenditure either to allow them to do more marketing in the places that are working or to try other media that they didn't have the budget to try at the outset.

When evaluating the success of marketing media it is important to give it sufficient time to properly evaluate its success. If a franchisor advertises in a national newspaper, they may have to advertise in at least two issues before being in a position to properly evaluate its success. When exhibiting at a franchise exhibition the franchisor may have to wait six months after the event before they can evaluate its success, as many people take a long time to decide on which franchise to buy. As the national franchise exhibitions are infrequent, they may not be ready to buy a franchise at the time of the exhibition but still registered an interest in a franchise with a view to researching it further, so that they would be ready when the time was right. It is important to mark the relative success of each marketing activity on the franchise recruitment plan, as this way it will help identify the most effective marketing activities ensuring the franchisee recruitment marketing budget can be put to best use.

So when deciding the best ways of advertising a franchise there is no straight forward answer, as the answer will be different for each franchise dependent on their franchisee profile and budget. Often however a mixed media approach, where a franchisor uses a range of franchise and non franchise media, proves more effective than just marketing the franchise opportunity using one type of media.

WHEN A FRANCHISOR RECEIVES AN ENQUIRY, WHAT PROCESS SHOULD THEY ADOPT?

By Clive Sawyer, Managing Director, Business Options

The recruitment process should be tailored to fit the franchisee profile and the franchise recruitment marketing plan. Having developed both of these, a franchisor can start to develop all the forms, documents and letters required within the recruitment process. These forms, documents and letters are combined together to form the franchise recruitment pack.

The franchise recruitment pack should contain everything required to handle an initial enquiry right through to signing up a franchise. Typically a franchise recruitment pack will contain fifteen to twenty different pieces of recruitment material dependent on the recruitment process adopted and can include amongst others:

221

1. Franchise Recruitment Process Map
2. Franchise Enquiry Form
3. Franchise Brochure
4. Franchise Brochure Letter
5. Franchise Application Form
6. Franchise Application Form Letter
7. Invitation to a Franchise Interview Letter
8. Decline for a Franchise Interview Letter
9. Confirmation of a Franchise Interview Letter
10. Confidentiality Agreement
11. Franchise Disclosure Pack
12. Provisional Franchise Offer Letter
13. Franchise Rejection Letter
14. Deposit Agreement
15. Deposit Agreement Letter
16. Franchise Agreement
17. Franchise Agreement Letter
18. Reference Request Letter
19. Formal Franchise Offer Letter
20. Franchise Training Confirmation Letter

Franchise Recruitment Process Map:

The Franchise Process Map is a flow chart showing the process an applicant will go through, referencing each document that will be required contained within the Franchise Recruitment pack.

There will be many steps in the franchise process some of which may have a number of different options, such as continue to the next step in the recruitment process; decide not to take the application any further; or additional information is required before proceeding. At each step the franchise recruitment process, the process map should state what the relevant course of action is and whether any document or form is required, and if so where in the franchise recruitment pack the document or form can be found.

By following a systemised process for franchisee recruitment, it will ensure that a franchisee receives all the relevant information at the right time that they will need to make a valued judgment as to whether the franchise is right for them. It will also ensure that the franchisor receives all the necessary information to decide whether the applicant is suitable as a franchisee.

Follow a systemised process for franchisee recruitment

Franchise Enquiry Form:

The franchise enquiry form is normally placed on the franchisors website so that a prospective franchisee can complete basic information regarding themselves to enable the franchisor to send them details about the franchise opportunity. The objective of the franchise enquiry form is not to qualify prospective applicants rather to enable the franchisor to start a dialogue with the interested person.

The enquiry form is the start of the franchisee recruitment process. It is important not to discourage any prospective franchisee at this stage. I have seen some enquiry forms that are five pages long and ask for a huge amount of information before the franchisor will send the person any information. It is important to remember that this may well be the first contact that the franchisee will have had with the franchisor and therefore first impressions are very important.

Franchise Brochure:

The franchise brochure, also referred to as the franchise prospectus, is primarily a high level summary of the franchise and does not contain any confidential information. The purpose of the franchise brochure in my view is as much about weeding out those people who the franchise is totally unsuitable for as it is about promoting the franchise. Normally franchise brochures are constructed to convey the following information:

The franchise prospectus, is a high level summary of the franchise

- What is the franchise about and what would a franchisee do
- How much does the franchise cost and what do they get for their money
- How much are they likely to earn if they are a franchisee
- The type of person most suited to be a franchisee, in other words a summary of your franchisee profile
- Answers to frequently asked questions such as is finance available, how long is the training, what ongoing fees does a franchisee pay, are the franchisee earnings guaranteed.

By providing this information, it should deter those people who do not want to do the role the franchisee will required to undertake, find the franchise too expensive, the earning potential is insufficient, or don't meet the necessary requirements.

Franchise Brochure Letter:

Regardless as to whether a franchisor posts or emails their franchise brochure it is important that the brochure is accompanied either by a letter or an email thanking the person for their enquiry and explaining what they need to do if on reading the franchise brochure they want to continue with their application.

Franchise Application Form:

For those people that have requested a franchise brochure and on receiving it still want to continue with their application, the next step in the recruitment process should be for the franchisor to collect more in-depth information on the applicant. This will allow the franchisor to decide whether the applicant meets their franchisee profile and it is worth from the franchisors perspective to continue with the application.

Having a standard franchise application form will ensure that the appropriate information is collected on each applicant to allow the franchisor to assess the applicant's suitability. Typically a franchise application form will be made up of seven sections:

1. Detailed personal information about the applicant such as address, contact details, marital status
2. Educational background and qualifications
3. Employment history
4. Financial status indicating whether they will need to borrow to finance their franchise and details of their bank for future references
5. Personal referee contact details
6. Questions about their suitability to be a franchisee
7. Space for the applicant to provide any other relevant information that they would like the franchisor to consider.

Franchise Application Form Letter:

When sending the franchise application form it should be accompanied by a letter or email providing instructions on how the applicant should complete the application form and what they need to do once it is completed.

The application form process should be the same for all applicants. Therefore it should be possible to create an application form letter or email that can be used when sending all application forms. Having a standard letter or email will prevent the franchisor from having to construct a new letter or email each time saving time and ensuring a consistent message is conveyed.

Invitation to a Franchise Interview Letter:

On receipt of a completed application form, the franchisor will need to make a judgement as to whether the applicant meets the franchise profile. If having reviewed the application form the franchisor believes the applicant may be suitable as a franchisee, then the next step should be to invite the applicant to an interview. The interview will be an opportunity for the applicant to find out more about the franchise and will enable the franchisor to further assess the applicant's suitability as a franchisee. The interview letter should explain what format the interview will take, where it will be held and how long it will last.

Decline for a Franchise Interview Letter:

If on receipt of the completed application form the applicant clearly doesn't meet the franchise profile the franchisor should reject the application. The franchisor should not be tempted to pursue the application on the off chance that the applicant may be suitable with additional training or support.

Therefore where the franchisor does not wish to take the application any further it is important to inform the applicant of the decision. It is normally best in these situations to keep the decline letter brief and to the point. The franchisor should not give detailed reasons for their decision as all this will do is give the applicant a reason to try and object to the decision.

Keep the decline letter brief and to the point

Confirmation of a Franchise Interview Letter:

Once a date for the franchise interview has been arranged it is good practice for the franchisor to write to the applicant and confirm the details for the interview. This ensures that there is no confusion regarding the format or purpose of the interview.

The franchise interview letter will also normally have a confidentiality agreement attached to it. The franchise interview letter should explain that at the interview the franchisor will need to provide the applicant with confidential information so that they can make an informed decision about the franchise opportunity. As this information is confidential the franchisor will require the applicant to sign the confidential agreement and return it to the franchisor in advance of the meeting.

Confidentiality Agreement:

The confidentiality agreement is a legal document and therefore it is important that it is created by a suitable qualified person. The confidentiality agreement will state that the information that the applicant is provided with must be kept confidential and can only be used by the applicant to assess whether to become a franchisee or not. None of the information is allowed to be shown or discussed with anyone that has not signed a copy of the confidentiality agreement. It will also state that on the franchisor request, the applicant must destroy all confidential information that they are in possession of and confirm in writing that this has been done.

Prospective franchisees should not have an issue signing a confidentiality agreement as it shows that the franchisor is taking the necessary precautions to protect the confidential information bout

Prospective franchisees should sign a confidentiality agreement

the franchise which, should it become public knowledge, could damage the franchise brand and effect the business of their franchisees.

Franchise Disclosure Pack:

At the franchise interview, the applicant will need to be told everything about the franchise opportunity in order to assess whether the franchise is right for them. In order to ensure that all relevant information is given to an applicant, it is normal to provide the applicant with a Franchise Disclosure Pack. Unlike some other countries where there is specific legislation that dictates what information must be disclosed to an applicant and in what format, in the UK there is no such requirement.

As there is no legal requirement in the UK as to what information should be provided to prospective franchisees, Franchise Disclosure Packs vary greatly in their structure. However if a franchisor is to provide a prospective franchisee with the information they will need in order to make a valued judgement as to whether the franchise is right for them, I believe that there are certain basic information that all Franchise Disclosure Packs should contain:

1. Background on the franchisors business
2. Assessment of the market that the franchisor operates within

3. Details relating to the Franchise Package; what it costs and what a franchisee gets for their money

4. Details relating to the key terms of the franchise such as how long the franchise is for, what happens if a franchisee wants to renew, the ongoing fees a franchisee will pay, the legal status that a franchisee must operate under, whether the franchisee will operate from home or commercial premises, whether a franchisee has to register for VAT before commencing their business, the policy regarding national accounts and any other key franchise terms

5. Explanation about the franchise territories, whether they are offered on an exclusive or non exclusive basis, and the criteria used to create a territory

6. Any minimum performance requirements that the franchisee must meet such as minimum income levels, minimum local marketing spend, or any other minimum performance criteria relevant to the franchise

7. The obligations that the franchisee must meet

8. The obligations that the franchisor must meet

9. The franchisee profile including any skills or experience that all franchisees must posses

10. A SWOT analysis explaining the Strengths, Weaknesses, Opportunities and Threats of the franchise

11. Detailed monthly and annual franchisee financial projections

The franchise disclosure pack is given to the applicant at the interview and they should be permitted to write on it and take it away with them. This is why it is essential that the applicant has signed a confidentiality agreement before being given the Franchise Disclosure Pack.

Provisional Franchise Offer Letter:

If following the franchise interview the franchisor believes that the applicant is suitable to be a franchisee then many franchisors will offer the applicant a provisional franchise, subject to suitable references being received and the applicant being happy to sign the franchise agreement. The provisional franchise letter needs to state what the conditions of the provisional offer are and what the applicant needs to do if they wish to accept the offer.

Franchise Rejection Letter

If following the franchise interview the franchisor decides that the applicant is not suitable to be a franchisee then the franchisor needs to write and inform the person of their decision. There is no requirement for the franchisor to provide reasons for their decision not to pursue their application any further. Therefore a brief letter thanking them for attending the interview but informing them that they have been unsuccessful in the application and wishing them every success in finding a suitable franchise can suffice.

Deposit Agreement:

As with the Confidentiality Agreement, the Deposit Agreement is a legal document and therefore should be produced by a suitable qualified individual. The Deposit Agreement will acknowledge that the deposit has been paid and specify the territory that the deposit relates to. It will also outline the conditions under which the Deposit Agreement is paid. It is important that the applicant signs and dates the Deposit Agreement and returns it to the franchisor for their records.

Deposit Agreement Letter:

The Deposit Agreement letter accompanies the Deposit Agreement and explains what the applicant should do with the Deposit Agreement should they wish to accept the provisional offer. It is also normal for the Deposit Agreement letter to highlight the key conditions under which the deposit is made as well as stating how and in what format the deposit should be paid.

Franchise Agreement:

The Franchise Agreement is the contractual agreement between the franchisor and franchisee and lists in detail all the terms under which the franchise is granted. Once the Deposit Agreement has been signed and the deposit paid then the franchisor will send the applicant the Franchise Agreement. It is worth stating that some franchisors do away with the deposit and Deposit Agreement preferring to send the Franchise Agreement to all applicants they feel are suitable as franchisees.

It is worth stressing that the Franchise Agreement should not be sent to prospective franchisees as a discussion document. It is important that all franchisees, wherever possible sign up to the same franchise agreement. This ensures consistency across the franchise network and makes it easier for the franchisor to monitor and enforce compliance across the whole network. If in exceptional circumstances a change is required to the Franchise Agreement for a specific franchisee, this should be done in the form of a side letter attached to the standard franchise agreement stating what clause has been changed and what the changes are. Franchisors should visit the temptation to make the changes directly to the original franchise agreement.

Franchise Agreement Letter:

The franchise agreement letter accompanies the Franchise Agreement and explains what the prospective franchisee should do with the agreement. It should advise them to seek legal advice from a specialist franchise solicitor so that they understand what they are signing and their obligations. The franchise agreement letter should also state that the franchise is conditional upon the franchisor receiving suitable personal references on

The Franchise Agreement is the contractual agreement between the franchisor and franchisee

the prospective franchisee and asking their written confirmation to contact the people listed as referees in the original franchise application form.

Reference Request Letter:

Although many franchisors decide not to take personal references on their prospective franchisees, I believe that it is a step in the recruitment process that should not be missed out. The personal references are the last check that a franchisor has before they allow a prospective franchisee to sign the franchise agreement. If a reference comes back unsatisfactory or the applicant refuses to allow the franchisor to contact the named referees then this may be reason for the franchisor to take additional steps to verify the prospective franchisees suitability.

Formal Franchise Offer Letter:

If the applicant's references are appropriate then the franchisor will send a formal offer letter. This formal offer letter will stipulate who the offer is made to and the territory it relates to. It will also explain the process that the applicant needs go through to accept the offer, which is normally to sign the Franchise Agreement and pay the Franchise fee less any deposit made.

Franchise Training Confirmation Letter:

This is the final document in the franchise recruitment pack. This letter confirms to the applicant that they are now a franchisee. It should also list the date, time, duration and venue of the franchisee training and any preparation the franchisee should do before they attend their franchisee training.

The franchise recruitment process.

As stated earlier, there is no legislation in the UK that dictates the recruitment process that franchisors should adopt. Having said this I am a strong believer that franchisors should follow a standard process for all applicants and provide them with all the information required so that an applicant can make a valued judgement as to whether the franchise is right for them. It is far better that unsuitable applicants are turned away at the earliest juncture, as it saves both the franchisors and the applicant's time and money. A detailed formalised franchise recruitment process with all the relevant forms and documents contained within the franchise recruitment pack is essential for a good franchise recruitment process.

Franchisors should follow a standard process for all applicants

HOW EXTENSIVE SHOULD A FRANCHISEE TRAINING PROGRAMME BE?

By Clive Sawyer, Managing Director, Business Options

Once a person has signed the franchise agreement and paid their franchise fees, the last step in the franchise recruitment process is getting the franchisee ready to start trading. This will involve training the franchisee in all aspects of the franchise business as well getting the franchisee set-up to start trading,

Franchisee Training:

The most critical step in ensuring that a franchisee is going to be successful and operate according to the rules of the franchisor is the franchisee training. The content, length and format of the franchisee training will vary for each franchise however the franchisee training should cover as a minimum:

1. How to run a business
2. The technical elements of the product or service the franchisee will sell
3. Franchise specific requirements

Part 1 – How to run a business:

The whole nature of franchising is that franchisees run their own businesses. This means that regardless as to the product or service their business sells, franchisees need to understand how to run and operate a successful business.

Many people who become franchisees have little business experience and therefore it is important that the franchisor provides appropriate training. For franchisees, this business training should cover four key elements:

1. Finance
2. Legal and Compliance
3. Staff
4. Back Office Systems

Finance:

Under finance, franchisees should be trained on the importance of having update to date financial information and how to use and interpret the information for the benefit of their business. In many franchises, franchisees are either discouraged or prevented from doing their own bookkeeping. This is because franchisors want their franchisees to spend as much of their time as possible focused on income generating tasks. Some franchisors provide a bookkeeping service for their franchisees, which most will charge separately for. Other franchisors will coordinate an outsourced chargeable bookkeeping service, and others leave it up to the franchisee to source their own local bookkeepers.

It is important that franchisees how to keep track of how their business is performing

Whichever approach is taken, it is important that franchisees understand the need to analyse the financial reports and how to do this to keep track of how their business is performing and what actions need to be taken to address any weaknesses in the financial performance of their business. The franchisee training should focus on how to interpret financial reports and how to identify strengths and weaknesses in the financial performance of the business so that appropriate action can be taken. Many of the customer management software systems used by franchisors will create reports on all aspects of a franchisees business.

Compliance:

There are many legal, regulatory and general business requirements that a franchise business, like any other business needs to undertake and comply with. These requirements can include:

- Creating the legal entity that the business is going to trade under, such as Sole Trader, Partnership or Limited Company
- Informing the relevant authorities that the business has been created
- Registering for VAT and filing VAT returns
- Registering as a data controller to comply with the Data Protection Act
- Taking out the necessary insurance required by the franchise business
- Setting up a business bank account and other banking services

Many franchisees will not have done these tasks before. It is therefore important that the franchisor provides training in all these aspects, to ensure each franchisee is set-up correctly from the outset. When we talk about training the franchisee, the training does not have to be done just by the franchisor. It is perfectly acceptable, and often better, that certain training is undertaken by external professionals.

> *Ensure each franchisee is set-up correctly from the outset*

Staff:
Some franchises will require the franchisee to employ staff.

Where this is the case, the franchisee will need to be trained on how to recruit, train and manage their staff. If all the franchisees in a network are going to operate in the same way, it is important that all staff within the franchise business are right for the job they are expected to perform and have been correctly trained. In order that this can happen the franchisor will need to train the franchisee on how to recruit the right staff for the right job. This is likely to include how to advertise, interview and select staff. The franchisee will also need to know how to comply with employment law regarding job descriptions, employment contracts and a raft of other employment legislation.

If a franchise is going to be successful the franchisee will also need to know how to manage their staff correctly. This may include how to communicate with staff effectively, how to monitor staff performance and give feedback, what to do when staff issues arise, and how to motivate and get the best out of their staff.

Some franchisors will make membership of an external employment advisory service a condition of the franchise. This ensures the franchisee will be able to access professional employment advice at any time enabling them to

Franchisees need to be trained to understand what their legal requirements are

comply with all employment legislation. Other franchisors will provide ongoing advice to their franchisees with regards to employment advice. Whatever approach is taken, franchisees need to be trained to understand what their legal requirements are when they employ staff and the policies and procedures that the franchisor wants the franchisee to follow in the training and management of their staff.

Back Office Systems:

For most franchises, the franchisee will be required to use the same proven back office systems and process as used by the franchisor. These back office systems will vary from franchise to franchise, however if a franchisee is going to use the systems correctly then they will require training on them.

Some franchisors use systems that have been specifically created for them. In these cases it will either be down to the franchisor to train the franchisee or the company that developed the systems in the first place. Where a franchise uses systems that are more generic and commonly available, it is normal that the franchisor will provide basic training on the system, and any additional training that the franchisee wants will provided by external providers/trainers, at the franchisees own cost.

Whichever approach to back office system training a franchisor adopts, it should be supported by a detailed user manual. This can either be incorporated within the Franchise Operations Manual, or can be a stand alone manual. It is unrealistic to expect any franchisee to remember everything that they are taught on their training course and therefore any training must be supported by a user manual that they can refer to, as necessary.

Part 2 – The technical elements of the product or service the franchisee will sell:

This section of the franchisee training is concerned with how to sell and deliver the products and services of the franchised business. This technical element of the training is normally broken down into three parts:

1. How to market the products and services
2. How to sell the products and service
3. How to deliver/install the products and services

Marketing the franchise business:
When a person buys a franchise they are buying into a proven business model. This proven model will include how to effectively market the products and services of the business. If no one knows that the franchised business exists, or is not aware of the different products and services that it sells, then it is unrealistic to expect the business to be successful.

In most businesses, franchised or not, there will be a wide range of different ways that the products or services of the business could be marketed. Business owners over the years will try different marketing mediums to greater or less success. This is the same for the franchisor. Not every bit of marketing they tried over the years will have worked. When a person buys a franchise they are buying into the knowledge and experience of the franchisor. This includes what the most effective ways to market the products and services of the business are. Without training in the most effective ways to market the franchisees products and services, the franchisee is likely to waste time and money trying various marketing approaches that the franchisor, from prior experience, already knows are not effective.

> *When a person buys a franchise they are buying into the knowledge and experience of the franchisor*

When training a franchisee on how best to market their products and services, it is important to acknowledge that there may need to be slight adjustment in the marketing undertaken to take into account local factors. A franchisor may have had little success in the past with advertising their services in local papers or at local networking groups. However it may be that in a certain franchise territory there is a very good local paper and very good local networking groups. Conversely the franchisor may have had success will local radio advertising however, in the franchisees territory the local radio station is less effective for businesses. It is for this reason that the franchisee training should include a section on what marketing has worked in the franchisors experience as well as how to research and evaluate the different marketing media in a franchisees local area. The franchisee should then develop their own local marketing plan based on what they have learnt from the franchisor and their own local research. They should then share this information with the franchisor allowing the franchisor to provide feedback and advice prior to them implementing their local marketing plan.

Selling the products/services:

Franchisors will have developed their own approach on how to sell to customers. This will include what happens when a customer lead is received through to how to convert the lead into a sale. The sales process for an oven cleaning franchise will be very different from a cost reduction business services sale. However, whatever the business is, the franchisee needs to be trained in the successful sales process that relates to their franchise.

A common mistake made by franchisors is that they train their franchisees on the technical nature of the business, such as all the different types of products in their range, but neglect to train them on the sales process leaving it up to the franchisee to sell in their own way. There are two key problems with this approach:

Firstly the franchisee may not be very good at selling. If this is the case the franchisee is likely to covert fewer of the enquiries into actual sales, which will affect the franchisees profitability and in turn will affect the franchisor, either in reduced franchisor fees or by making it harder to sell franchises in the future due to having failing existing franchisees.

Secondly, there is a risk to the brand integrity if franchisees are allowed to sell in whatever way they like. If a network has ten franchisees all selling as they see fit, it is likely that all ten will adopt slightly different methods. Some of these sales methods may be very good and be effective however there may be some that are either ineffective or worse damage the

There is a risk to the brand integrity if franchisees are allowed to sell in whatever way they like

reputation of the franchisors brand. The only way to ensure consistency throughout a franchise network is to train every franchisee how to sell using the franchisor's proven method and to then monitor the franchisees to ensure that they sell the way they have been trained.

Delivering and installing products and services:

For most franchises, once the franchisee has sold a product or service they will need to deliver or install it. If a franchisee sells a corporate training course, it likely that they will have to run the training course for the customer. If a franchisee has a fast food take away business, then once they have a customer who wants to buy their burger, the franchisee needs to make sure the food is cooked and wrapped for the customer to take away.

This element of the technical training is normally the most extensive part of the franchisees training. The franchisee will need to know every part of the delivery and installation process if they are going to deliver and install the product or service in exactly the same way, every time. If a franchisor has a chimney sweep business the franchisee will need to know every piece of equipment that they require, how to set each piece up, how to operate the equipment, how to deal with any issues or problems that can occur, how to check the cleaning has been done properly and how to tidy up after themselves. If a franchisor has a flower arranging franchise then the franchisee will need to know all the different flowers that can be used, the sizes of arrangements that can be made, how to arrange the flowers, and how to package and deliver the flowers to the customer.

As with all parts of the franchisee training, if a franchisor wants their franchisees to deliver and install the products and services they sell exactly how they want them to, then franchisees must be properly trained. Franchisees must also be provided with detailed instruction manuals covering every part of the process so that they can refer to it any time required. If a customer visits a McDonald's, they know, regardless as to whether they love the food or not, that the Big Mac will taste the same whichever McDonald's they visit. Franchisors need to train their franchisees so that whichever franchisee delivers their products or services, and which ever part of the country they are in, the customer will get the same consistent result.

Part 3 – Franchise specific requirements:

In franchising, unlike most traditional businesses, franchised businesses have a unique extra element to them. This involves franchisees regularly reporting back to the franchisor with their performance results and paying the variety of franchise fees due to the franchisor.

If a franchisor wants all their franchisees to report back the same way, they must be trained how to do it. Franchisees will need to be trained in what reports are required and the frequency. Some franchises such as those in the fast foods industry,

Franchisees will need to be trained in what reports are required and the frequency

often require franchisees to report back to the franchisor on a weekly basis. Other franchises only require them to report back on a monthly basis. Whatever frequency adopted, the reason for franchisee feedback should be twofold:

1. To know how the franchisee is performing so that the franchisor can give support, advice and where necessary additional training to help the franchisee improve.
2. To be able to calculate the fees to charge the franchisee.

The franchisee needs to be trained in what information they will need to provide the franchisor, the frequency they need to provide it and in what format. A fast food franchise may require more extensive reports more frequently from their franchisees than a dog grooming franchise. Whatever level of information and frequency of reporting a franchisor chooses it is important to make it simple for the franchisee to provide it. Some franchisor systems will create this information automatically. Other reports are partly automated and partly rely on the franchisee completing a manual return. Where the franchisee is going to have to complete a manual return it is important that they understand why the information is required. If a franchisor asks for the number of enquiries received in a month and the number that converted into sales, it is important that they explain why the information is needed. As long as it is explained to the franchisees that there is a typical conversion rate perceived as normal within the business and that a lower level than this may indicate a potential issue, the franchisee will understand the need for supplying this information. If however a franchisor asks franchisees to report on the type and make of every car they wash in the car washing franchisee, but don't explain why this is required, then it is likely that some of their franchisees will be reluctant to collect and provide the information.

When I explain this to franchisors, some respond that franchisees have no choice in this matter and must provide the information requested, as the franchise agreement states they must do it. However running a franchise based on threats of legal action for things the franchisee does not consider reasonable will only lead to unhappy, disgruntled and less productive franchisees. In contrast, having happy motivated franchisees is the same as having happy motivated staff, they are far easier to manage and far more likely to perform to a higher

Running a franchise based on threats of legal action will only lead to unhappy franchisees

level than unhappy disgruntled ones. Therefore, if there is a reason to collect information the franchisor should explain the reason for it to their franchisees. If there is no specific reason to collect specific information they should not ask for it.

However, whatever information a franchisor asks for, their franchisees need to be trained on how to collect it, when to collect it, in what format, and how to send it to them.

For paying franchisor fees, the franchisee will need to be trained on how to calculate the fees due, how to pay them and when. In some franchises the franchisor will calculate the fees due themselves and inform their franchises the amount due. However, even in these cases it is still important that the franchisee understands how the fees are calculated and can verify the amounts due.

Once fees have been calculated by the franchisor or the franchisee, the franchisor needs to be paid. This can be done a number of ways, but typically as a direct debit or by bank transfer. Franchisee will need to know whether payment is due a certain number of days after the month end or in the case of the franchisee purchasing products from the franchisor, due when the franchisee places an order. Whatever payment method is adopted, the franchisee will need to be trained how to do it.

How extensive should a franchisee training programme be?

Without wishing to endlessly repeat the same point, the only way for a franchisor to ensure that every franchisee in their franchise network runs their business exactly the same way is by providing them with detailed training in all aspects of the business. This training should be supported by a comprehensive Franchise Operations Manual and supporting guides and manuals that the franchisee can refer to. There is no standard duration for franchisee training as it all depends how long it will take to train a franchisee in every aspect of the business.

WHAT INFORMATION SHOULD BE IN A FRANCHISE OPERATIONS MANUAL AND HOW PRESCRIPTIVE SHOULD IT BE?

By Clive Sawyer, Managing Director, Business Options

The Franchise Operations Manual is a critical element of any franchise. The Franchise Operations Manual provides all the detailed instructions on how a franchisee *must* operate their business and along with the Franchise Agreement forms the legal conditions under which the franchisee will operate.

When considering how much detail to include within a Franchise Operations Manual, the answer is very straight forward, it is as detailed as it needs to be to ensure that every franchisee operates in exactly the same way. Unfortunately most Franchise Operations Manuals do not go into sufficient detail. The reason often given by franchisors is that they want their franchisees to take ownership of their franchise, and therefore they don't want to be too prescriptive. However this can be a major mistake.

If one asks ten people to do the same task, it is very likely that they will do it in ten slightly different ways. When the franchisor's brand integrity is in the hands of its franchisees, franchisors should take all necessary steps to prevent one of more franchises doing anything which could damage its reputation. A franchisor also has a responsibility to protect their franchisees' investment as franchisees would not be happy if the franchisor allowed one franchisee to damage the franchise brand which will ultimately affect them all.

> *The franchisor's brand integrity is in the hands of its franchisees*

The only way to ensure that every franchisee operates in exactly the same way is to leave nothing to interpretation. The Franchise Operations Manual has to state, in minute detail, everything a franchisee should do and how they should do it.

As a Franchise Operations Manual covers every part of the franchisees business, and given that every business is slightly different, there is no such thing as a template Franchise Operations Manual. The only real use of a template Franchise Operations Man-

> *There is no such thing as a template Franchise Operations Manual*

ual is to provide general topic headings that can be used as a check list against the franchisor's bespoke Franchise Operations Manual.

Having said that every Franchise Operations Manual is different, there two distinct parts:

1. Setting up and running a franchised business
2. Selling and delivering the products and services of the company.

Part One – Setting up and running a franchised business

Some of the most common areas included within this section of a Franchise Operations Manual are:

1. Key contacts that the franchisee will need, when to contact them, and their contact details
2. A statement saying that the franchisor owns the copyright of the Franchise Operations Manual
3. Instructions on how to use the Franchise Operations Manual and the process for updating it
4. What the franchisee needs to do when setting up their franchise, such as company formation, VAT registration, data protection registration, the different insurances they will require etc.

5. Instructions of Health & Safety compliance
6. The process for employing and managing franchisee staff
7. Training staff and ongoing franchisee training
8. Office layout, equipment and signage rules
9. Dress code policy
10. Vehicle type, livery, maintenance and usage policies
11. Telephone usage and policy
12. Email format and usage
13. Accounts and bookkeeping procedures
14. Franchisee reporting requirements
15. Franchise territory rules
16. National accounts policy and procedure
17. The process for recommending improvements to products, services and internal systems
18. National and local marketing policies and instructions
19. Marketing material that is available to franchisees
20. National marketing campaigns procedures
21. Instructions on how to order branded products such as stationery and marketing material
22. Franchisor and franchisee website policies

In addition to providing detailed instructions for all these areas, the Franchise Operations Manual will also need to contain copies of every form, document, template and guide that a franchisee may need to use.

Part Two – Selling and delivering the products and services of the company

This section will state in minute detail how the franchisee must sell and deliver their services and products. Typically it will cover all the stages in the customer sales transaction, such as:

1. How to handle enquiries
2. What to do at customer meetings
3. How to create customer quotations
4. How to process customer orders
5. Taking customer payment
6. Delivering the service or product
7. Post sales follow up process
8. What forms and documents to use and at what step of the sales process
9. What levels of stock a franchisee should maintain
10. Customer complaints procedure

Most franchised business will have some form of computerised customer records system. Within the Franchise Operations Manual, detailed instructions on how to enter information onto these computerised systems should be provided. Often franchisors will include screen prints of every step coupled with instruction notes, as it is only

Include screen prints of every step coupled with instruction notes

through this level of detail and information can the franchisor be confident that the franchisee will follow the process exactly.

Another useful tool when creating this part of a Franchise Operations Manual is to include process flow charts for each stage of the sales process. Often flow charts are easier to follow than long paragraphs of text.

Online versus hardcopy

A question I frequently asked in relation to the Franchise Operations Manual is what format the Franchise Operations Manual should be provided in, hardcopy or online. I come from the old school view that many people prefer to have a hard copy that they can refer to, but there are pro's and con's for each approach.

An online version is easier to update centrally and allows a franchisee to access the Franchise Operations Manual anywhere they can get internet access. The downside is that franchisees still have a tendency to print off key sections of their online Franchise Operations Manual and forget to update them when sections are changed. This means that there is a risk that they end up referring to a Franchise Operations Manual that is out of date.

A hard copy version makes it easier to ensure every Franchise

Operations Manual is the same as each time there is a change a new page is sent to the franchisee; however this is more time consuming for the franchisor. The downside is that Franchise Operations Manuals are large documents and often stay on a franchisees shelf as they are not practical to carry around.

As modern technology continues to develop, I am sure that the days of hard copy Franchise Operations Manuals will be numbered. When a franchisor is considering what format to provide their Franchise Operations Manual, the best advice is to think about who is going to use it. If the majority of their franchisees are over 50 years of age, there may be an

Think about who is going to use it.

argument to use a hard copy format as the older the franchisee is, the more likely they are to feel comfortable with a hard copy version. Conversely if all their franchisees are young, it is likely that they have grown up with the internet and will feel more comfortable with an online version. Whichever version is adopted, it is worth being prepared as inevitably, some franchisees within a network will want to use the "other" format, unless both formats are offered!

What information should be in a Franchise Operations Manual and how prescriptive should it be?

The Franchise Operations Manual should cover every element of the business in minute detail. Nothing should be left to the interpretation of individual franchisees. It is only by having such a comprehensive detailed Franchise Operations Manual that the franchisor can protect the integrity of their brand and the investment of their franchisees.

HOW MUCH SUPPORT SHOULD A FRANCHISOR GIVE THEIR FRANCHISEES?

By Clive Sawyer, Managing Director, Business Options

For any business that wants to have a successful franchise network, the hard work really starts once they have recruited and trained their franchisees and their franchisees start to run their franchised businesses. Unfortunately some franchisors take a different approach and believe that once they have recruited and trained their franchisees the hard work has been done and they can leave their franchisees alone and watch their franchises fees start rolling in.

The success of any franchise network relies on all franchisees following the instructions in the Franchise Operations Manual exactly and all operating in exactly the same way. When anyone attends a training course, regardless of the topic or complexity, it is

It is virtually impossible to remember absolutely everything taught

virtually impossible to remember absolutely everything that they were taught. Even with supporting training guides and handouts that a person can refer to at a later stage, it would be unrealistic to expect anyone to operate and get everything totally correct. In this respect franchise training is no different. The initial franchisee training and the supporting Franchise Operations Manual is only the first step in ensuring all franchisees in a network operate successfully in exactly the same way. The initial training and the Franchise Operations Manual need to be supported and reinforced by:

1.   Regular performance monitoring
2.   Ongoing training
3.   Regular communication

Regular Performance Monitoring:

If a franchisor is to know whether all of their franchisees are operating in exactly the same way and are in compliance with the terms of both their franchise agreement and the their Franchise Operations Manual, the franchisor will need to instigate a range of systems and processes to enable them to monitor what their franchisees are doing.

A standard clause within a Franchise Agreement will make it mandatory for a franchisee to provide certain information to their franchisor on the performance of their business. This requirement will be explained in detail within the Franchise Operations Manual and will state what information has to be provided, in what format, and at when. Having this information on each franchisee will enable the franchisor to remotely monitor their franchisees performance and identify any issues that may need addressing. This however should only be one part of the performance monitoring undertaken by the franchisor.

One big problem for a franchisor that purely relies on their weekly or monthly franchisee reports for monitoring their franchisees performance is that the reports are only as good as the information they contain. Where a franchisee report is completed manually by the franchisee, they can intentionally or unintentionally omit certain information that will mean that the franchisor does not have a true picture of how they are performing. Even automated franchisee reporting systems are open to abuse. An automated system is only as good as the information it contains. A franchisee may decide not to record certain information that they may believe will reflect badly on them. Therefore any good franchisee performance monitoring system must substantiate the franchise reports with independent verification processes. These processes could involve monthly

> *Reports are only as good as the information they contain*

franchisor visits to observe the franchisee in action. The verification process may also involve independent mystery shopping exercises or independent audits. Whatever verification processes are adopted they must, together with the franchisees reports, enable the franchisor to have an accurate picture of exactly how each of their franchisees are performing. Only then can a franchisor help their franchisees address any areas where they may be falling down. This will help the franchisees to be more successful, which will in turn help protect the franchisors brands integrity and increase the franchisors income from ongoing fees and increased franchisee recruitment.

Ongoing Training:

Ongoing training is an essential part of any successful franchise operation and is used for three main reasons:

1. Addressing knowledge gaps
2. Reinforcing key points within the business
3. Learning new skills

Addressing gaps in a franchisee's knowledge, identified through the franchisors performance monitoring systems and processes, is probably the most obvious reason for undertaking ongoing franchisee training. As previously stated, it is unreasonable to expect anyone to remember absolutely everything they are taught on a training course. Even with supporting manuals and guides that a franchisee can refer to, there is no guarantee that a franchisee will perform every task the way it should be done. A franchisee may incorrectly think they remember how they were taught to do a task and therefore not check whether they are doing it correctly. Alternatively a franchisee may refer to their Franchise Operations Manual or a supporting guide to check that they are doing a task correctly only to misinterpret the instructions contained in the manual. Although Franchise Operations Manuals and guides should be written in a way to try to ensure that they are simple to understand and minimise the risk of misinterpretation, it is inevitable that people will make mistakes. Therefore ongoing training can be used to address any gaps and misunderstandings in a franchisee's knowledge.

It is inevitable that people will make mistakes

There may also be certain key parts of a franchise business that franchisees may need to be continually reminded of there significance. It may be that a franchised business has a unique selling point when compared against their competitors. For example, a hand car washing franchise not only washes the outside of the car but will also clean the internal door sills as a free added extra service. If this makes the business stand out from the competition, the franchisor must ensure that their franchisees do not cut corners and omit to do this or perhaps when they are busy, that they mistakenly believe that it is more important to get to the cars that are queuing to be cleaned as quickly as possible rather than spend the extra couple of minutes cleaning the inside door sills. This franchisees monthly report may not identify this, or when their franchisor visits them it may not be their busy period and therefore do not cut any corners. Therefore, in these instances, getting franchisees together to reinforce the importance of key elements of the business is critical. Not only can a franchisor reinforce key points but it will allow them to address any issues raised by their franchisees. If a franchisee disagrees with the importance of doing the extra task or the Unique Selling Point and ongoing reinforcement training will allow the franchisor to address their concern. Often this reinforcement training is undertaken with groups of franchisees at the same time, other franchisees can reinforce the benefit of doing the task properly.

When a person buys a franchise they are normally entering a long term commitment. Typically franchises are for five years with options to renew. This means that it is likely that a franchisee will be operating their business for at least ten years. If one compares the products and services a business offers today against those they offered ten years ago, I am sure in virtually every business there will have been some changes. Any business that is going to remain competitive needs to react to changes in market conditions. This may mean introducing new products and services to compete with the competition or it may be that improvements are made in the way things are done. Whatever the reason, franchise businesses are the same as non franchised businesses and must continually look at ways to improve what they are currently doing for the services and products they offer.

In a franchise, this research and development of new systems, processes, products and services is undertaken by the franchisor. The franchisor should develop and test new products, services and procedures and when they are ready, role them out through their franchisee network. As these will be new to the franchisees the franchisor must bring their franchisees

The franchisor should develop and test new products, services and procedures

together to explain the reasons for the new products, service or procedures and then train them on their use.

I have referred to three different reasons for ongoing franchisees training. But it is important to remember that training can take many different forms. Getting franchisees in a room to train them all together is the most appropriate way however there are other ways to do this, such as, interactive learning material which may include the use of DVD's and online training modules or perhaps a video conference may be more appropriate. It is important to choose the most appropriate training medium

> *Choose the most appropriate training medium for both the franchised business and their franchisees*

for both the franchised business and their franchisees. Whatever approaches a franchisor take, ongoing training is an essential part of establishing a successful franchise network.

Regular Communication:

The final part of successful franchise management relates to regular communication. As with any relationship, whether between a boss and an employee, individual family members or a franchisor and a franchisee, regular communication is essential.

For a franchise to be successful it is essential that the franchisor and franchisee work together towards a common goal. The franchisee needs to believe that the franchisor has their best interest at heart. If they believe this is the case, they are more likely to be motivated in the way they run their franchise compared with if they believe they are working alone without the support or interest of the franchisor.

Regular communication will also provide opportunities for issues to be raised and addressed at an early stage before they are able to escalate into a bigger issue. Although some franchisees may believe that regular communication with their franchisor is unnecessary and too time consuming as it takes them away from their business, it is the franchisor's contractual responsibility to help and support their franchisees. If the franchisor is going to be effective in the way they help and support their franchisees, they must have regular contact with them.

Regular communication however does not have to mean face to face meetings. Face to face meetings are a very good way of communicating between people, however telephone calls, video conferencing, emails, circulars and even texting can be good ways of maintaining contact between a franchisor and their franchisees. A telephone call just to see how a franchisee is doing may provide the opportunity for a franchisee to raise an issue with their franchisor which otherwise would not have been mentioned.

It is the franchisor's contractual responsibility to help and support their franchisees

It is too easy for franchisors to take the line that the franchisee has their contact details and therefore can contact them whenever they like. In realty if a franchisee doesn't feel that the issue is big enough to warrant contacting the franchisor themselves, the issue is unlikely to go away and is more likely to fester and become larger. By telephoning the franchisee, it may give them the opportunity to raise the issue and have it resolved. This will enable the franchisee to them get back to running their franchised business.

How much support should a franchisor give their franchisees?

I hope it is clear that a franchisors work really starts once they have trained their franchisees and they have started their business. If a franchise network is to be successful, the franchisor must know how each of their franchisees is performing and have processes in place to allow issues to be addressed and improvements to be rolled out. Every business is different and therefore the amount of time and approach to supporting franchisees will differ between franchises. However franchisors should not underestimate the time and resource required to support franchisees properly and should budget accordingly from the outset.

CAN A FRANCHISEE SELL THEIR BUSINESS AND WHAT IS THE PROCESS?

By Derrick Simpson, Managing Director, Franchise Resales Limited

For the vast majority of franchisees in the UK the answer to this question is a clear yes; they are able to sell their businesses when they wish to. The reason I have qualified the direct answer to the question is that the relationship between a franchisee and their franchisor is enshrined within the franchise agreement between them and the right for a franchisee to do anything at all pertaining to the sale of their business should be provided for, or not, within that agreement.

> *The vast majority of franchisees are able to sell their businesses when they wish to*

The majority of franchise agreements will contain a clause, in some form or other, which will provide the right of a franchisee to sell their business at some stage. This however is not an automatic facility and there will be some franchisors agreements that do not provide for the sale of a business. In these circumstances, at the end of the agreement, the franchisee will be expected to either re-sign the current version of the franchise agreement for another term, hand the business back to the franchisor or simply close and cease to trade. In other words they are only able to make a return on their business whilst actually operating it – not as part of an eventual business sale.

In my view not providing the right for a franchisee to sell is an unethical stance for a franchisor to adopt. The British Franchise Association (bfa) will not admit any franchisor as a member that prevents its franchisees being able to benefit from their time in their network and capitalising the value of the business they have established.

Franchisors that restrict franchisee resales are very much in the minority in the UK – though they do exist. Prospective purchasers of any franchise are strongly advised by consultants, the franchise units of banks, the bfa and other franchise professionals to seek legal advice from a solicitor specialising in franchising and one that is an affiliated member of the bfa. Taking this step ensures purchasers are made fully aware of their obligations under the franchise agreement so are able to decide for themselves whether to go ahead with a particular franchisor or not. A bfa affiliated solicitor will clearly point out any lack of a resale provision in a franchise agreement. Franchisors considering an approach to franchising with a franchise agreement that restricts the ability for their franchisees to eventually sell-on their business are advised to speak with a bfa affiliated consultant and solicitor to ensure these business options and their implications are clearly explained to them.

By far the vast majority of franchisors however do allow their franchisees to sell their businesses and many enlightened ones will actively encourage their franchisees to be thinking and planning towards this eventuality. This Exit Planning approach to franchisee support delivers mutually beneficial results as both parties are "singing from the same song sheet" and the focus is on developing a successful business for franchisees.

The right to sell

The outline of the process to be followed by a franchisee wishing to sell a business within a particular franchise network will be set out in the franchise agreement. This section sets out the options open to the franchisee and will most usually describe the broad actions to be taken with a resale and how the franchisor will wish to be involved, or not, in the process. This section will also usually set out any costs or fees payable by the selling franchisee upon sale and the fees payable by the purchaser to the franchisor over and above the price paid for the business they are acquiring.

The franchise agreement will however only cover the basics of the process to be followed and is the "fall-back position" of the franchisor. The detail of the process to be followed and any operational advice for the selling franchisee would, or should, be set out in the operations manual as part of the general operating processes of the franchise.

Plan for a resale

Franchisees should be encouraged to start out in business with the view to sell on their business at some stage. If they have a focus on their "end game" and the requirements of a resale such as profit and sales growth on a consistent basis, they will run an altogether more efficient and successful business than franchisees without such a focus.

Start out with the view to sell the business at some stage

There are many elements that influence the final achieved selling price of a business which can be put into place at the time of launching the business that may be difficult to change later. Whether to purchase or lease equipment and vehicles, whether to rent or buy property, employing a number of family members; all will have an effect on the ability to eventually sell and therefore, usually, the price to be achieved.

This process cannot start early enough and many franchisors use part of the recruitment interview process to discuss the eventual sale of the franchisees business. This is the correct approach as it fixes in the mind of the prospective franchisee from day one that there is a life-cycle within the franchise and they can, eventually, sell on. The risk however is that this is where the discussions are left and the topic of selling is then not mentioned again.

There should always be the gentle reminder to franchisees of this life-cycle within the franchise. Many franchisors will do this through business planning meetings or annual reviews. In this way franchisees are able to keep in mind that they need to be developing their businesses on a daily basis and this in turn grows the franchisors flow of Management Service Fees (MSF) or product sales if the franchise operates in this fashion. There is less of a direct benefit to franchisors that only charge a fixed monthly fee though the benefit to the franchisee will be the same.

Many franchisors supplement this general focus on the final sale of a business with structured Exit Planning seminars delivered from time to time at annual conferences. Whilst these are usually the more established franchisors there is no reason why a newly established franchisor shouldn't build this type of session into their support programme.

Establish a resales process

There is of course no point in discussing the eventual sale of a franchisees business if the franchisor does not have a structured resales process in place. Even newly launched franchisors will come across early franchisees that decide, for whatever reason, that they wish to go. It is sensible therefore to have the process in place from day one or use an outsourced provider to pick up any early resales that occur.

A resales process should provide guidance to franchisees on how to go about the process of selling, how much the franchisor will become involved in the process and any constraints on the franchisee. The process should also detail fees payable by the selling franchisee and the purchaser and may well provide guidance on how to establish a fair value for the business. There may also be examples of the required documentation and advice on the planning and execution of the resale.

Many franchisors will outsource their entire resales process rather than trying to manage the odd one or two resales themselves but however this happens the entire process involved should be written down and openly provided to franchisees. The best place to provide the resales

Many franchisors will outsource their entire resales process

process to franchisees is as a "Guide to Selling your Franchise" within their Operations Manual. The reason to place the Guide to Selling here is that it is then seen to be part of the franchisors system. This removes any mystique or uncertainty about the process and franchisees can see that this is simply part of their life-cycle within the franchisors network.

Documentation

In addition to the "Guide" describing the resales process it is useful for franchisors to have their own templated pro-forma Prospectus of Sale (Information Memorandum) for franchisees to complete when they wish to sell. If the franchisor creates this template they are able to ensure it contains the correct description of the franchisors business and may even add a description of their "ideal" candidate. The rest of the document will then detail the type of information that the selling franchisee needs to provide and leaves blank spaces for them to add this data. It is important that the franchisee provides this information, rather than the franchisor doing this for them, because in this way there is no risk of the franchisor being open to any accusation of manipulating or distorting the information. Possibly an unlikely occurrence but in this regard I advocate a "better be safe than sorry" policy.

These are the areas of information that a selling franchisee should be encouraged to provide. They will vary from franchise network to franchise network because they will each operate in a different fashion. Some will be home based, others premises based with staff etc, whilst others may be vehicle based. All will require different information.

It is important to have as much detailed information as possible about each individual resale because if a prospective purchaser has to wait whilst the selling franchisee scrabbles around looking for detail to respond to questions it is likely they will become bored and go elsewhere. In my experience it is important not only to excite a prospective purchaser in a particular opportunity, it is also important to retain their interest whist they consider their options.

> *It is important to excite a prospective purchaser*

These therefore are the main sections of a structured Prospectus of Sale / Information Memorandum:

- Overview of the franchise
- History of the specific business
- Sales figures
- Details of the territory
- Any property or staff involved
- The operating profitability

- List of assets and details of any operating leases
- What is being sold (ltd co or assets and goodwill only)
- Asking price
- Reason for sale
- Copies of audited/certified accounts

If the above is available in the correct format then the selling franchisee has a good chance of securing a purchaser. Certainly any prospective purchaser will at some stage in the process require all the above detail to enable them to make a decision about whether to purchase and at what level to pitch an offer. Clearly if the information isn't available they will be unable or may be unwilling to take that step and decide to buy.

The legal side

Once a sale is agreed there will be a legal completion process, just as with any other commercial sale or house sale. A contract of sale or Sale and Purchase Agreement (SPA) is prepared, agreed between the parties, documents are exchanged, training of the new franchisee takes place and the sale completes following training when the new franchisee takes over.

It is quite possible to allow the selling franchisee and their purchaser to organise their own solicitors and SPA. It may seem like a good idea not to be involved but the franchisor needs to protect their brand and the detail of how the transfer of the business occurs. So it is now becoming the norm for a franchisor to have their own solicitor draft a templated SPA which is then passed out by the franchisors "managing solicitor" to the purchasers and sellers solicitors to work with. Many will actually become a part to the agreement because in doing this the franchisor can stipulate any clauses within the SPA that they would not allow to be altered – a point franchisors should discuss with their solicitors. These would relate to the protection of their brand and also any practical issues that, from their experience, would complicate the transaction. The detail of the sale terms between seller and purchaser would not be involved, just the clauses that reflect on the brand and the network as a whole. Naturally the franchisors solicitor would have a fee for carrying out this work and it would be usual for this fee to be fixed and split between the purchaser and seller. The rationale being franchisors shouldn't have to incur additional costs to help a franchisee sell their business.

By creating a transparent process a franchisor is showing there is nothing wrong with planning to sell a franchise

The whole system

A truly effective resales system is one that is clear and easily understood by all parties in-volved. By creating a transparent process a franchisor is showing there is nothing wrong with planning to sell a franchise and that it is in fact a natural part of business life.

These are the main elements of an effective resales process

- Guide to selling for vendors
- Guidance for purchasers
- Exit planning process
- Valuation guidance
- Pro-forma prospectus of sale
- Pro-forma sale and purchase agreement
- Dedicated franchisor solicitor

All part of the operations manual

Why bother?

More and more prospective franchisees investigating a future business opportunity are actively seeking an existing business to buy rather than starting from scratch. The bfa survey of UK franchising published in 2011 showed that 36 percent of franchisees purchased their franchise as a resale. This means that fran-

36 percent of franchisees purchased their franchise as a resale

chisors, whilst still wishing to expand their brand through organic growth must also take into account the large number of prospective purchasers that would take on a resale if available.

By having a structured process to enable franchisees that wish to move on to be able to do so a franchisor will be creating a true win-win situation. Without a process in place the franchisee wishing to sell would most likely, after a period, start to loose motivation and decline in performance and this could cause a strain on the franchisee/franchisor relationship. Having a structured route for them to follow demonstrates that, as part of the franchisors support processes, there is a way out when they want one. A purchaser can take on a running business with all the added advantages that derive from this and the franchisor will have a rejuvenated business as the new franchisee takes the business to a new level.

The logic is clear. The application does require some detailed planning and probably qualified external advice from a bfa accredited resales specialist but the net result will be an enhanced franchise support process that will demonstrate to franchisees, new and old alike that the franchisor is supporting them throughout their life with the franchise network.

Changes to recruitment and training

Having established a system for allowing franchisees to sell or deciding to outsource the process it is important for franchisor to consider what changes, if any, they need to make to their systems and processes to support resales.

Depending on what is the key function of a franchisee – are they sales based, service deliverers or a manager of others – there may be the requirement to modify some part of the franchisors recruitment, training, launch and initial support processes.

In a new "greenfield" location with a new franchise one of the main success drivers will be the ability to seek new clients and develop the business rapidly – a hunter gatherer approach. With a resale, however, there will already be a customer base so the key requirement will be relationship building and nurturing of the existing business to secure it and develop it further – a farming approach. It may be the franchisor will need to seek purchasers with a slightly different skill set for a resale opportunity than a new location. This will clearly depend on the type of operation it is but the principle remains that one size may not fit all in every case.

Then there is the induction training. Most franchisors have their training courses set up for new franchises in new locations. When a purchaser of a resale joins such a course will all the information and training be relevant? If so fine, but if not, the course may need altering here and there.

Most franchisors will assist their new franchisees to launch their businesses. With a resale there is no launch – it already exists – so the mechanic of that process may need to be different for a resale.

All of these aspects need to be considered because at some stage they will arise and if thought has been applied and answers formulated in advance solutions can be provided for most of eventualities involved with a resales transaction.

The resales of existing franchised businesses are here to stay. Franchisors need to be prepared for this from day one so they can act confidently and provide considered advice to franchisees. This will build franchisees confidence in their franchisors and enhance the ongoing franchisee/ franchisor relationship as well provide the potential for addi-

> *The resales of existing franchised businesses are here to stay*

tional franchisor income. As with all aspects involving the establishment and operation of a franchise, the best advice on the resales process will always be provided by a franchise resales professional affiliated to the bfa.

CAN A FRANCHISOR SELL THEIR BUSINESS AND WHAT ARE THE PITFALLS?

By Derrick Simpson, Managing Director, Franchise Resales Limited

A franchisors business is the same as any other commercial venture and therefore is able to be sold and ownership transferred in just the same way as other businesses. There are of course different structures involved in the operation of a franchisors business and I will deal with these differences and the effects they have below. To directly answer the first part of the chapter heading however, the answer is 'yes' a franchisor can sell their

> *'Yes' a franchisor can sell their business*

business. Many franchisors have sold in the past and many more will do so in the future. As with any business sale the ease and smoothness of the eventual sale will, in the most part, depend on the way the business is operated from the start. It is therefore logical for a franchisor to plan their eventual exit at the very beginning – just as it is good practice to advise franchisees to do.

Before deciding on an eventual exit route or its timings it is important for a franchisor to consider fully their options because these will vary over time as will the potential value achievable from the sale of their business.

If a franchisors business is to be sold successfully it needs to attract its target purchasers. Not only must a prospective purchaser see the opportunity or reason to acquire a particular network they also must be able go through the due diligence and legal processes involved with the minimum of cost and hassle. Long drawn out purchase processes will often fail to complete. Franchisor sales where everything is in place and transparent are quicker to complete and will often attract a higher selling price because they may be deemed more organised and thus more desirable.

> *Franchisor sales where everything is in place and transparent are quicker to complete*

Saleability

One of the first points to consider is the overall saleability of the business. I am sure all franchisors believe their particular businesses are fantastic and very attractive so why shouldn't any purchaser be prepared to pay top dollar for the opportunity to buy it? A fair question to ask but a franchisor should consider where they are in the development of their business and how this reflects on its attractiveness to a purchaser in terms of both desirability and value.

All commercial enterprises can be valued and the value will usually be based upon their ability to generate sustainable returns on the investment – *EBDITA or put simply how profitable they are. There is also the opportunity element to take into account. Is there development and growth potential? Are there synergies between the buyers existing business and the potential acquisition? Can the potential purchaser see opportunities for cost reduction, streamlining or integration with another business? All of these can add to the businesses attractiveness and are additional decision forming factors.

> *All commercial enterprises can be valued and the value will usually be based upon how profitable they are*

Taking 'development potential' as an example. A franchisors business that has 10 or so franchisees will clearly have the potential to grow further as more franchisees come on board. But does this mean a purchaser would pay a premium to acquire this – probably not. A fledgling franchisors business will

---

*EBITDA (Earnings Before Interest Tax Depreciation and Amortisation)

not generate much profit so will require the purchaser to invest further in the business to grow it. Add that to the low existing profit generation and the answer is that a business that is under developed is most likely not that valuable.

At the other end of the scale a franchisors network that is full or has sold all of its available territories has no where else to go in terms of new sales growth. They may be a profitable franchisor but where does a purchaser obtain their future revenue growth? There could be territory splits, a driven resales programme to take on new franchisees whilst losing some of the longer term ones currently in place, possibly some form of streamlined combining with an existing business. All possible but all requiring vision and effort from the purchaser therefore making the business less attractive or valuable.

Timing the franchisors sale is therefore important. Making the business attractive in terms of profitability but still providing scope for future growth and development.

Franchise Agreements

Franchisor businesses have one distinct difference to other commercial trading ventures and that is their franchisees. Franchisees, or rather their Franchise Agreements, are key assets of the business. Franchise agreements are legal contracts that define a trading relationship between franchisee and franchisor which would be transferred to a new owner as part of a franchisor sale. Just because franchise agreements are pieces of paper, rather than tangible pieces of equipment or infrastructure it doesn't make them any less valuable. In fact it

The franchise agreements may well be the most valuable assets of the business

can be argued that within a franchisors business the franchise agreements may well be the most valuable of the assets of the business.

Best practice in managing franchise agreements correctly from day one is, in my view, vital.

- Ensure the franchise agreements awarded all include a clause that provides the right for the franchisor to sell or assign the agreement to a third party. Without this a franchisor may have difficulty selling their business.
- Create a register of signed franchise agreements giving the franchisees details, the date the agreement was signed and the version of the franchise agreement involved.
- Have a register of franchise agreement versions. Each change made to an agreement should generate a different version number. This register should list the

versions and the variations from the original, ideally with an example agreement attached. This register will then easily cross reference to the overall franchise agreement register. This and the first point above may seem like a lot of additional effort but this advice is provided to ensure a smooth eventual business sale without vast legal expenses being incurred during any due diligence process.

- It is important to ensure franchises do not run out of their agreement and carry on trading un-regulated. Monitoring the FA register will ensure agreements are not allowed to lapse. Whilst it can be argued that by continuing to trade within a franchise network and paying fees that fall due any franchisee with a lapsed agreement could be deemed to have accepted the on-going terms; why get into that position in the first place when simple administrative housekeeping can prevent this from occurring.

- Never adjust or make changes to a franchise agreement to suit an individual franchisee. Franchisors with a tendency to make one-of changes to agreements will simply cause confusion with a multiplicity of versions in use and will vastly overcomplicate any due diligence being carried out by a purchaser. In fact this action alone may make the franchisors business unsaleable due to the complexity created.

- There can be a temptation to vary some franchise agreements with a side letter for specific franchisees usually to encourage recruitment. This should be avoided because it once again creates a complex situation.

- The wider point to note, and with reference to all the points above, is the importance of getting the terms of the franchise agreement correct in the first instance. It is for this reason that franchisors are advised to only work with experienced, bfa accredited solicitors to draft franchise agreements. Getting this right at the outset saves time and money later.

- Always ensure any changes to an agreement are made in conjunction with the franchisors solicitor so they have been advised on the effect such changes may have.

- Even if a franchisor doesn't think their agreement requires any changes it is good franchise practice to have an annual review of the agreement with their solicitor to ensure it is always up to date with both, best practice, the ethics of franchising and the law.

- As far as possible try to ensure there are not too many agreements expiring at the same time. This is difficult to control but a franchisor should consider the simple error made in the case study below.

Franchise Agreement Case Study

This case study illustrates the potential dangers of not planning ahead and operating a franchisors business with the eventual exit process in mind.

A UK franchisor had a master licence from the US which ran for an initial 25 year term renewable in 5 yearly tranches thereafter. When they launched in the UK and commenced selling franchises they awarded franchise agreements ending on the same date as the initial term of the master agreement. At the time it was considered the ethical way to act as there was no guarantee the ML would be extended beyond that end date. When part-way through the master licence period the master licence was rolled on 5 years the franchisor extended their own franchise agreement by that period and moved the end date for new franchisees to the new master licence date. In effect they then had two franchise agreements one terminating on each ML termination date. This seemed fine because incoming franchisees felt they had additional security through having a long term to their agreement and this very fact aided the franchisors recruitment and growth.

The franchisor grew well over the years but realised, eventually, they had dozens of franchisees with agreements all terminating on the same date in two blocks 5 years apart. The risk to the franchisors business is clear to see. This was a situation that could have been avoided with forethought about the potential result of this strategy and correct initial advice. It was a situation that was only resolved through an extensive programme of franchise resales – issuing new agreements to the new franchises – and negotiations with the remaining franchisees once they reached the end of their original agreements based on franchise terms up to 25 years old. The ML was re-negotiated going forward on a different basis.

It is hard to see how a business sale would have been constructed if that franchisor had been involved in one prior to putting their house in order.

Executive Staff

It is likely that a franchisor will have developed a business over a number of years before considering a sale. It is equally likely that during that time a number of staff will have joined and many will be holding key positions within the franchise operation. Founders of franchised businesses will often eventually step back from the day to day management of their network and bring on senior executives to take on the major and time consuming tasks. These are usually the franchise facing and operational elements or finance roles.

Founders of franchised businesses will often step back from the day to day management

293

At the time of preparing to sell the franchise network it is important to also consider individual executives as assets of the business. It is unlikely that a purchaser of a franchisors business is going to want to dive into the detail of the day to day operations, they are more likely to want to have the business run on an on-going basis by the team currently in place. There are always going to be exceptions to this but generally this will be the case.

If senior managers are to be considered assets of the business it is important therefore that they are secure. An investor seeking the acquisition of an on-going operation will want to see that the executive team are not able to "up sticks and leave" on a whim. I know of many employed Directors of franchised companies on 30 day notice employment contracts because the owner of the business is keen not to have their hands tied if they ever decide to remove the individual. This however can be seen as a negative in the eyes of prospective purchaser. So there is a balance to be struck between having employment contracts that prevent people leaving instantly and locking them in for so long that the asset becomes a liability.

A key point is to ensure that all staff are covered by signed contracts of employment relative to their value to the business.

Other Potential Issues

Property Leases: Many franchisors run networks that operate out of premises. How these properties are held will have an effect on the sale process. This will also vary depending on the industry sector in which the franchisor operates.

Many Quick Service Restaurants (QSR) or Fast Food franchisors will hold property leases themselves, or through a specific allied property company, and sublet locations to franchisees. This because they consider franchisees holding property leases a risk and wish to secure the location of their outlets as this encourages future trade through location awareness. To a prospective purchaser of a QSR or Fast Food franchisor having control of the location of the outlets can be seen as a strength of the business as it restricts the ability of franchisees to relocate or close and lose the site from the network.

In complete contrast this scenario in a non-location specific franchise would be seen as a liability to a purchaser because if a franchisee failed the franchisor would be left with an on-going lease liability. The decision therefore on who holds the property lease depends on the industry within which the franchise operates.

Supplier Contracts: If the franchisor has contracts with suppliers, as opposed to arrangements for franchisees to contract with suppliers directly, it is important these are up to date and fully documented. Franchisors usually only have supply contracts themselves if the product or service involved is core to the operation of the franchise. This being the case it is likely to be part of the requirement of a sale that such contracts are current and on-going. If supplier contracts are not vital then best practice would be for contracts to be between franchisees and nominated suppliers

Litigation: Clearly all businesses wish to avoid litigation but it does happen. In planning a sale it is important to have the details of past legal actions documented and available for the due diligence process. Any current legal challenges by or against the franchisor must be declared.

Any current legal challenges by or against the franchisor must be declared

Accounts – both annual and management: One hopes that this paragraph is superfluous however experience tells another tale. Accounts for a business being prepared for sale must be clear, unencumbered by complex business structures and, most of all, current. It is pointless considering a business sale without up to date accounts.

The layout and detail of the accounts needs to be clear so the purchaser is comfortable and therefore more likely to continue. Presenting sets of accounts that require reams of notes explaining the various elements will simply serve to put off suitors. This is where adequate planning and preparation is required to structure accounts in a logical transparent and understandable fashion. Presenting muddled accounts and expecting a purchaser to plough through the detail is to risk losing them.

Up to date management accounts provide current detail giving comfort to prospective purchasers that the business continues to perform in line with, or better than, previous audited results. Both historic audited and up to date management accounts as well as coherent cashflow projections are required to achieve a successful sale.

Intellectual Property and IP Rights: The assets of the business being prepared for sale also include the intellectual property of that business and the rights to its use. With a master licence franchise that is being sold the owner of the IP and the right to use it will be the ultimate franchisor that has granted the ML agreement. In these cases the IP rights etc will be licensed to the new owners of that business through a re-issued or assigned master licence agreement.

For wholly owned franchisor businesses a prospective purchaser will wish to see that Trade Marks are owned and registered, at the very least, for EU operation and ideally throughout the world. The selling franchisor must be the owner of websites and the knowhow that drives the individual franchisees businesses, licenced to them through their franchise agreements, as these are also part of any sale.

A key part of the preparation for any business sale therefore is to ensure that all Intellectual Property and the rights to its use are transferable with the sale.

Target Purchasers

When instigating the process of selling a franchisors business it is useful to understand who may be interested in the acquisition and therefore who to target. I use the term target deliberately because if a vendor is aware of their audience and any Prospectus describing the business is focussed to that end there is a far greater chance of success. Simply casting out into the general business sale marketplace with a "please buy me" message is likely to be less successful.

Management Buy Outs are a popular way of achieving a transfer of the business

MBO: Many franchisor sales have been made to the management teams then in place in the business. Management Buy Outs are a popular way of achieving a transfer of the business and are likely to be supported by funding institutions. The reason they work is that the purchasing person, or team of people, will be familiar with the system and operating processes they are acquiring. They will be known by the franchisees and staff so there is a greater likelihood of a smooth transition and successful future growth. Funding institutions will be encouraged because of these positives.

From a sellers perspective an MBO may be a quicker sales process because the purchasers will be familiar with the business and whilst a due diligence process will take place; it should be a quicker and simpler process than with an external purchaser. On the negative side an MBO may deliver a lower achieved selling price or require a programme of phased payments. This can occur because the employees involved may not have accumulated enough liquid capital or have adequate assets to secure the required funds to pay the agreed price in full. In this instance a business owner may take the view to proceed with the sale on a phased payment process and take a further step back in the business whilst still remaining a shareholder to protect their future income payments.

Even though MBO purchasers may have adequate capital, they may feel they were the people involved in creating the value within the business and so question why they should pay as much.

A complication can occur with an MBO if the proposed sale fails. This could lead to a strained relationship between the parties involved which could result in the senior member or members of staff leaving the business. The selling franchisor must look at the pro's and con's of an MBO process and decide if the team they place is able and interested in an MBO and if not perhaps they should create a management team that would be.

Trade Sale: Another logical target for the selling franchisor is a business sale to a company within a similar arena or where the acquisition of the business for sale would add value to the combined organisation.

Cluster franchisor operations, with multiple brands owned by one umbrella company, are becoming more common because this allows economies of scale to be applied to the combined organisation. Central services such as recruitment, accounting, legal services and distribution all supporting a number of operating brands can make cluster franchising a very attractive business option. A specialist broker working in the franchise arena would target other franchisor organisations, especially those that had already a two or three brand operation, to interest them in investigating another.

A further option may be a supplier seeking access to a wider target market that might look at acquiring a franchise operation as a way of reaching a wider consumer audience.

If the purchasing business or person is keen to acquire the franchisors business it is quite possible to achieve a higher sales price with a trade sale. This is particularly where there are strong synergistic elements between the businesses.

A trade sale is a less transparent process than an MBO and will usually require a specialist broker to bring the sale to fruition. A Prospectus of Sale or Information Memorandum will be required to attract prospective purchasers and the due diligence will be a detailed affair. This means a sale would need to be kept confidential, have progressed well to agreement and be secure before a selling franchisor is able to speak to their staff and franchisees about what is happening.

> *A trade sale is a less transparent process than an MBO*

Private Equity Investment and/or Floatation: As time has progressed private equity investors have taken a greater interest in the franchise sector. Several of the larger UK franchise brands are owned by private equity companies and this trend seems to be increasing. The reason for this is the ability to grow a franchised business through the recruitment of new franchises or cluster franchising which provides growth and the opportunity to exit with a capital gain.

Most PE investor companies will wish to dispose of their

investment within a five year or so period so the business will be expected to grow well in that period for them to be able to achieve their goal. Usually a PE investor will agree, in advance, a sale process with the vendor franchisor and agree an earn-out formula after an agreed term which will give the owner their exit route. The PE investors will usually not invest much cash but leverage debt and will require business efficiencies as the term progresses to ensure their planned exit can be achieved. Private equity investors usually aim to realise their investment either through a trade sale or via a stock market floatation.

A franchisor that has been used to total autonomy whilst running their business may find a private equity process restricting. The investors will usually take a Board position and will have the ultimate say in major decisions such as investment and senior staff appointments. The selling franchisor will be contractually tied into the relationship for the term if they wish to achieve their price. This process will suit some franchisors but not all.

The floatation of a franchised business on one of the stock markets, usually Plus Markets or AIM, is not common. The markets have yet to understand the true value of franchised businesses and whilst there have been one or two successfully carried out these are usually large operations with well know brand names. In most cases it is the brand name of the franchise and not the business concept that attracts investment. For smaller franchisors floatation can be an expensive, drawn out and complex route that has no guaranteed successful outcome; though when it works it usually works well.

> *The floatation of a franchised business is not common*

Planning

Throughout this entire chapter the underlying theme has been to plan ahead. There is a lot to prepare in any business sale and a franchisors business is no exception. My advice is to ideally plan for the eventual sale of the business at the point of inception and at least three years in advance of a target sale.

Selling a franchisors business can be an emotional roller coaster. Most franchisors have established their business from scratch. They have worked hard to establish and grow the franchise. They have nurtured the franchisees, often becoming friends in the process. Once going down the sale route the emotional element can be hard. There may be false starts, prospective purchasers backing out or confidentialities breached. It is hard work to prepare all the documentation and due diligence investigative detail a purchaser will require. Above all however the sale process is a distraction from the day to day operation of the business so one to be approached with care and by taking experienced professional help from a bfa affiliated advisor.

This chapter does not cover the legal elements of a franchisor sale because the process is the same as for any other commercial sale. The non-legal elements are covered above and getting these key points correct, from the outset, will provide a franchisor with a greater chance of a successful sale.

TOP TIPS

Treat your franchisees fairly

By Clive Sawyer, Managing Director, Business Options

If you can't commit fully to franchising don't do it

By Clive Sawyer, Managing Director, Business Options

Resist the temptation of signing up unsuitable people as your franchisees

By Clive Sawyer, Managing Director, Business Options

Seek guidance and support from experienced and reputable franchise professionals.

by Richard Holden, Head of Franchising, Lloyds Banking Group

Review your franchisee's business plan regularly

by Richard Holden, Head of Franchising, Lloyds Banking Group

Understand how bank managers think and what they consider when assessing a lending to a franchisee

by Richard Holden, Head of Franchising, Lloyds Banking Group

Keep it simple

By Jonathan Chadd, Partner, Head of Franchising, Leathes Prior Solicitors

Consider carefully what group benefits you can offer to your franchisees:

By Jonathan Chadd, Partner, Head of Franchising, Leathes Prior Solicitors

Get the best advice you can:

By Jonathan Chadd, Partner, Head of Franchising, Leathes Prior Solicitors

By Nicola Broadhurst, Partner, Head of Franchising, Stevens & Bolton Solicitors

Is the franchise concept proved?

By Nicola Broadhurst, Partner, Head of Franchising, Stevens & Bolton Solicitors

Can you afford it?

By Nicola Broadhurst, Partner, Head of Franchising, Stevens & Bolton Solicitors

Do not act as a Bank

When recruiting franchisees don't be afraid to say "No"

by Graeme Payne, Partner, Field Fisher Waterhouse LLP

Protecting a logo isn't enough to safeguard your trade marks
by Graeme Payne, Partner, Field Fisher Waterhouse LLP

Help your franchisees plan their eventual exit
by Derrick Simpson, Managing Director, Franchise Resales Limited

Business Planning support helps franchisees achieve their goals
by Derrick Simpson, Managing Director, Franchise Resales Limited

Run your business as if it is always for sale
by Derrick Simpson, Managing Director, Franchise Resales Limited

TOP TIPS FROM CLIVE SAWYER, MANAGING DIRECTOR, BUSINESS OPTIONS

- **Treat your franchisees fairly**
  If a franchise is going to be successfully it has to work for both the franchisor and their franchisees. Perceived fairness in the franchisor / franchisee relationship should exist in every element of the franchise from the fees the franchisee will be charged, the clauses in the Franchise Agreement, any minimum performance targets a franchisee may be required to meet, the approach to national account

business, through to the ability that franchisees have to suggest improvements. Franchising is like any other relationship, whether personal or business, if both parties feel the relationship is fair then it is likely to succeed, however if either party feels it is unfair then it will lead to resentment and ultimately a breakdown between the two parties. Structure your franchise to be fair from the outset.

- **If you can't commit fully to franchising don't do it**
Franchising a business involves time and money both in setting up the franchise and more importantly in supporting and managing a network of franchisees. Many businesses fail at the outset because they do not have the money to franchise properly and opt for the cheap enticing internet offers that say they can franchise a business for a cut price. As with most things in life taking short

Franchising done properly can provide an excellent way of expanding a brand

cuts often cost you more in the long run. Even when a business sets up their franchise properly failure is a real possibility if the franchisor is not prepared to commit the time and resources to support and manage their franchisees. Franchising done properly can provide an excellent way of expanding a brand regionally, nationally and internationally however done incorrectly it can be costly for both the franchisor and their franchisees. If you don't have the money and the time to commit to franchise properly either, don't franchise, or wait until you do.

- **Resist the temptation of signing up unsuitable people as your franchisees**

  I say this to every business owner when they start out of their franchisee recruitment and every business owner is adamant that they will only sign up suitable people who meet their ideal franchisee profile; however when a business starts to interview potential franchisees they realise that they are faced with a real dilemma. Having spent a significant amount of money setting up their franchise, there is often a need to start to recoup their investment by selling franchises. The franchisor is also faced with the problem that prospective franchisees are more attracted to franchises that have a network of franchisees to prove the concept rather than a franchise just starting out with no franchisees. Therefore signing up franchisees as quickly as possible, even though they may not be entirely suitable, is very tempting as it overcomes these two issues: it brings in some money to start repaying the initial investment in setting up the franchise and it also starts to

  > *The first franchisees will be the role models that other prospective franchisees will look to*

create the franchise network. However tempting this may be, be very careful. The first franchisees will be the role models that other prospective franchisees will look to. If your first franchisee(s) are not successful then this will have a dramatic effect on how other prospective franchisees view your franchise. In addition if the first few franchisees are not successful they are likely to take an excessive amount of your time and resource in managing them. Resist the temptation, and have the courage only to recruit people who are right for your business and meet your franchisee criteria.

TOP TIPS FROM RICHARD HOLDEN, HEAD OF FRANCHISING, LLOYDS BANKING GROUP

- **Seek guidance and support from experienced and reputable franchise professionals.**

  There are many pitfalls to avoid when franchising a business so it pays to set off on the right foot by using experienced and knowledgeable consultants and solicitors. The British Franchise Association accredits professionals who have demonstrated over time their expertise in supporting fran-

  Set off on the right foot by using experienced and knowledgeable consultants and solicitors

chisors develop their brands. Banks are more likely to provide financial support to a franchise and the franchisees investing in that brand if it has been developed with the assistance of bfa affiliated professionals.

- **Review your franchisee's business plan regularly**
  It is good practice for the franchisor to undertake regular reviews their franchisee's business plan and to ensure that it is updated as the business evolves. This can form the basis of discussions about the development of the business at review meetings. Most people consider a business plan is just needed to secure the financial backing they require from a lender however it is far more useful than that. The document should be used to benchmark where the business is against the financial projections and to identify areas that are not going according to plan. If business owners just waited until their accountant produces the end of year financial accounts to review what shape their business is in it may be too late by that time to put in place any recovery plans.

- **Understand how bank managers think and what they consider when assessing lending to a franchisee**
  Business owners and bank managers often think very differently. People who run their own business commonly have a degree of entrepreneurial spirit and are calculated risk takers whilst the typical bank manager is very conservative. When approaching a lender for financial assistance it is

important for the business owner to put themselves in the shoes of a bank manager and understand a proposition from their prospective. By doing so they will be able to prepare a stronger proposal and identify solutions to potential challenges the bank manager may raise.

TOP TIPS FROM JONATHAN CHADD, HEAD OF FRANCHISING AND IPR TEAM, LEATHES PRIOR SOLICITORS

- **Keep it simple**

  Franchisors should ensure that their lawyers provide them with clearly defined procedures to be followed on the issue of each franchise agreement to a new franchisee and to ensure that the franchisee fully understands the obligations he is taking on. These should include tailoring the standard form franchise agreement to particular circumstances of the transaction and keep the agreement up to date with changes in legislation or in the business system. They should cover company incorporation, VAT registration, data protection notification and premises acquisition. All the above should be addressed (where applicable) in a manner that ensures that the franchisor's interests are fully protected as well as those of the franchisee.

  > *Ensure that the franchisee fully understands the obligations he is taking on*

The correct property procedures should avoid delays in the acquisition of the lease of the premises and/or in the fit-out of the store. They should also, where relevant, retain for the franchisor the ability to take over the premises in the event of the termination or expiry without renewal of the franchise agreement.

- **Consider carefully what group benefits you can offer to your franchisees:**
  Franchisors should consider carefully the additional benefits they can offer their franchisees through the enhanced purchasing power and resources of a franchised network. Depending upon the type of business this may well include providing a cost effective solution to securing access to specialist employment law advice, health and safety policies and advice, discounted insurance premiums with standard form insurance policies tailored to the business risks as well as discounted arrangements with suppliers of products and services relevant to the business. The provision of such additional benefits to franchisees will bolster their enthusiasm for participation in the network and tie them ever more tightly into the franchise arrangement. A franchisee is far less likely to feel disgruntled about payment of the management service fee when he is the recipient of significant discounts on products or services that are all vital to the operation of his business. Franchisees who feel their franchisor is making every effort

to assist them in ways in which they, themselves, would not have considered and which improve the profitability of their business are likely to work hard to ensure not simply the success of their business but of the network as a whole.

- **Get the best advice you can:**

Select professional advisors who lead their field. The investment will be repaid many times over. Cutting corners on such advice is a big mistake that will ultimately cost you many times over. BFA affiliated professional advisors have many years of specialist franchising expertise, we have "been there before" and seen the scenarios you will encounter and be able to identify the best solutions for your business. In addition to offering specialist legal or consultancy advice they will have a wide range of personal contacts invaluable to your business and be able to offer sensible practical and commercial advice from their own experience.

> *Cutting corners is a big mistake that will ultimately cost you many times over*

TOP TIPS FROM NICOLA BROADHURST, PARTNER, HEAD OF FRANCHISING, STEVENS & BOLTON SOLICITORS

- **Is the franchise concept proved?**
  Although the BFA recommends that a pilot franchise operation should be run before a business concept is launched as a franchise this is often overlooked through impatience. A franchisor wishing to avoid claims of misrepresentation must ensure that all statements made to prospects are based on fact not fantasy and financial projections based on actual trading figures. A pilot operation provides the necessary evidence to determine the commercial viability of the franchised business.

  Ensure that all statements made to prospects are based on fact not fantasy

- **Can you afford it?**
  For a franchisee it is not just about the initial franchise fee. There will be other start up costs to consider and working capital is required. The cost is not just financial, starting a business takes time, energy and commitment all of which can take a toll on private life. Therefore it is essential that the family is behind the individual buying the franchise. A franchisor is well advised to interview prospects in their home or invite partners to interviews to assess the level of support that will be available.

- **Do not act as a Bank**

  It can be tempting for a franchisor to "help" a franchisee through tricky patches or with cash flow issues. One offs do not present too much of an issue. However prolonged help can set an unwelcome precedent together with an unrealistic level of expectation that can leave the franchisor financially exposed.

  A franchisor is not a bank and should not assume a credit risk for a franchisee

  A franchisor is not a bank and should not assume a credit risk for a franchisee. Franchisors supplying products should always retain flexibility to amend the credit terms offered to franchisees and practical sanctions to rectify non-payment by a franchisee.

TOP TIPS FROM GRAEME PAYNE, PARTNER, FIELD FISHER WATERHOUSE LLP

- **When recruiting franchisees don't be afraid to say "No"**

  Having advised a range of franchisors from individual entrepreneurs, medium sized businesses going through a re-engineering exercise to large multinational companies using franchising as a growth tool for international expansion, a common tip to emerge is: don't be afraid to say "no" when recruiting a potential franchisee. A number of franchise clients and contacts who with the benefit of hindsight have said "I wished we hadn't recruited so and so", "they nearly ruined our business" or "they killed our business in Reading/the Middle East/France etc" all comment that the best investment that they made (usually after a painful lesson or two) was looking at their recruitment process and procedures (or lack of) and making sure they selected the right franchisee for their business.

For aspiring franchisors, particularly small start up franchisors it will pay dividends many times over to say "no" to those franchisees who do not meet the franchisor's criteria or simply about whom the franchisor's gut instinct says "no". Whilst the injection of much needed capital, or the opportunity to grow the network or expand in a new territory

> *to say "no" to those franchisees who do not meet the criteria*

may be very attractive, if the franchisee turns out to be a nightmare, simply saying "no" can save a franchisor thousands of pounds, a considerable amount of time and maybe their business!

- **Protecting a logo isn't enough to safeguard your trade marks**
  A number of franchisors particularly at the start of their franchise journey will register their brand logo as a trade

mark by themselves in the interests of saving costs. This can be one of the most fundamental and expensive mistakes that a franchisor can make. As the brand is a key element of a franchise business, it is essential that both the logo and more importantly the word mark are registered as trade marks. Not only must the key logos and word marks be registered, but they must be registered in the correct products and services classes with a specification wide enough to protect the business as it grows.

A franchise business without brand protection is like a house without foundations. A franchisor who is not willing to invest the time and money in protecting its brand will be exposed to legal action from not only other brand owners who have correct protection but also from its franchise network. Without solid trade mark registrations a franchisor is unlikely to defend itself from such actions and runs the strong risk of losing its business as a whole.

A franchise business without brand protection is like a house without foundations

Investing in correct and thorough brand protection will not only allow a franchisor to expand with confidence but will also add significant value when the franchisor comes to sell.

318

**TOP TIPS FROM DERRICK SIMPSON, MANAGING
DIRECTOR, FRANCHISE RESALES LIMITED**

- **Help your franchisees plan their eventual exit**

  The whole methodology of franchising is based upon structured systems that allow franchisees to launch, develop and prosper from being part of a franchisors network. Franchisors have processes that help franchisees join a network and marketing systems and tools that help them grow their businesses. The step that most franchisors fail to provide is the help and support that enables franchisees to successfully sell and exit the network. Franchisors should be able to show their franchisees, from the day they join, how their activities will help them achieve an eventual profitable sale and have in place processes, or access to processes, that will enable franchises to do this. Having a structured exit process in place that dovetails into the ongoing business support provided can make the franchisor a more attractive option for potential franchisees. So planning franchisees exits can in fact help achieve greater franchisor growth.

  Provide support that enables franchisees to successfully sell and exit the network

- **Business Planning support helps franchisees achieve their goals**

  There can be a tendency amongst franchisors to think that the only time franchisees require detailed support is during their induction and launch period. Once they are trained to deliver whatever it is the network does the task is to then encourage/drive franchisees to grow for mutual benefit. Franchisors should take into account that franchisees do not usually arrive with a complete basket of business skills.

  Franchisees do not usually arrive with a complete basket of business skills

  Many will have a sales focus so may not be fully au fait with cashflow planning. Others may be financially sound but not that hot at marketing and sales. A regular business planning programme with franchisees will help them establish their goals and measure their success, develop a cashflow forecast to monitor and, if appropriate, recruit and motivate the right staff to work with. This combined approach will cement the franchisee/franchisor relationship and should generate profitable sale growth which will be a true win – win for all.

- **Run your business as if it is always for sale**

  Franchisors with even the slightest thought in their mind that they will eventually wish to sell their businesses are advised to operate them on a day to day basis as if they are already for sale. During day to day business operations it is quite easy to slip into bad habits or allow staff to do the same thing. Little things such as keeping a note of telephone conversations with franchisees, not responding fully to franchisee queries, not being quite as thorough with the selection of franchisees when there are recruitment targets to reach – all these are potential nails in the coffin of eventual sales. Franchising is a systematic process. Franchisors should have their own operating systems for the administration and operation of their franchisor business and ensure they are adhered to. This simple act will ensure any eventual sale will be that much simpler and smoother to complete.

FRANCHISE GLOSSARY
OF TERMS

BFA:

The British Franchise Association was established in 1978 with the aim of regulating franchising on an ethical basis, by granting membership to those franchisors that it considers, meets the demands of its Codes of Ethics and procedures.

Business Format:

The term used to describe a franchise where the franchisee buys into the total system of the brand, including the brand name, know-how, training, methodology, systems, procedures and ongoing product development.

Buy Back:

Where the franchisor agrees to purchase the franchise back from the franchisee where the franchisee no longer wishes to continue.

Disclosure: The practice of revealing detailed information about the franchisor's business and franchise package, prior to the signing of the Franchise Agreement. This is a legal obligation in many European and North American countries, although only voluntary in the UK.

Exclusive Territory: The area within which a franchisee will operate and where they are the only person within the franchisee network that is permitted to proactively market their products or services.

Franchise Licence: The right to operate a franchise using the franchisor's brand name system of the brand, know-how, methodology, systems, and procedures for which an initial Licence fee is charged as well as Ongoing Fees.

Franchise Contract: Often referred to as the Franchise Agreement, and sets out the terms under which the Franchise Licence is granted.

Franchise: The business format being offered for sale under a Franchise Licence.

Franchisee	The person or company buying the Franchise.
Franchisor:	The company selling the original Franchise and providing the support to their franchisees.
Franchise Package:	The goods and services that the franchisor will provide a franchisee, enabling them to launch their franchise business.
Intellectual Rights:	The franchisor's "secrets" of doing business including the various Trade Marks, Patents, Branding, Manuals etc.
Master Franchise:	A licence granted to an individual or company to operate in more than one territory; often Master franchises are granted for a whole Country or large Region.
Franchisor : Management Fee	Sometimes referred to as a "Royalty" or "Ongoing Fees". These are the fees that the franchisee will pay the franchisor, usually monthly, as a fixed amount or a percentage of the franchisee's turnover.
Operations Manual:	The detailed document or manual which describes every aspect of how the franchisee should run their franchise business.

P&L Projections: The calculations, based on the franchisor's experience, which predicts the franchisee's financial performance.

Pilot Operation: A test undertaken by the franchisor to assess how their franchise will operate and how successful it will be. The pilot is set-up in a separate geographic location and is run at arms distance from the franchisor to replicate how an independent franchisee should operate and perform.

Renewal: The legal provision for granting a further franchise term once the initial term has expired. Usually there are a range of conditions attached to any franchise renewal.

Re-sale: Refers to the sale of a franchise, by a franchisee, to another person or company other than the franchisor.

Royalties: Sometimes referred to as "Franchisor Management Fees" or "Ongoing Fees". These are the fees that the franchisee will pay the franchisor, usually monthly, as either a fixed amount or a percentage of the franchisee's turnover.

Term:	Refers to the length of time the franchise is granted for.
Termination:	The legal provision by which either party may terminate the Franchise Agreement, often used when the franchisee materially breaches the terms of the Franchise Agreement.
Trading Act:	Known as the Trading Schemes Act (1996). This was introduced to combat the maligned practice of "pyramid selling".
Vertical Block Exemption:	On 1st June 2010, revised European regulation came into force effecting Vertical Agreements, which are agreements entered into by parties at different levels of the supply chain, and which includes franchising. The Vertical Block Exemption exempts franchise agreements amongst others, from being restrictive agreements under Article 101 (ex Article 81) of the EU Treaty, so long as certain conditions are met.

SOURCES OF HELP

Listed below are a selection of organisations and sites that people considering franchising their business may find of help. Please note this is not an exhaustive list and there will be other places that there are other places where information can be found.

Selected Franchise Associations:

The British Franchise Association
British Franchise Association, Centurion Court, 85f Milton Park, Abingdon, OX14 4RY
Tel: 01235 820 470
Email: mailroom@thebfa.org
Web: www.thebfa.org

European Franchise Federation
179, ave. Louise, B-1050 Brussels, Belgium
Tel: 00 32 2 520 16 07
Email: info@eff-franchise.com
Web: www.eff-franchise.com

International Franchise Association
1350 New York Avenue NW #900, Washington DC 20005, USA
Tel: 001 202 628 8000
Email: info@franchise.org
Web: www.franchise.org

For a full list of franchise association's visit:
www.thebfa.org/international.asp

Banks with Dedicated Franchise Departments:

Lloyds Banking Group
Franchise Unit, 2nd Floor, Northgate House, Kingsway, Cardiff, CF10 4LD
Tel: 0800 587 2379
Email: franchising@lloydstsb.co.uk
Web: www.lloydstsb.com/franchising

HSBC
Franchise Unit, 12 Calthorpe Road, Birmingham, B15 1QZ
Tel: 0121 455 3438
Email: franchiseunit@hsbc.com
Web: www.hsbc.co.uk

NatWest

NatWest/RBS Franchise Team, 1st Floor, 280 Bishopsgate,
London, EC2M 4RB

Tel: 0800 092 917

Email: franchise.retailbanking@natwest.com

Web: www.natwest.com/business/services/market-expertise/
franchising.ashx

The Royal Bank of Scotland plc

RBS Franchise Section, Level 1, 280 Bishopsgate, London,
EC2M 4RB

Tel: 0800 092 917

Email: FranchiseRBS.RetailBanking@rbs.co.uk

Web: www.rbs.co.uk/business/banking/g3/franchising.ashx

Franchise Exhibition & Show Organisers:

Venture Marketing Group

Tel: 020 8394 5226

Email: adrian.goodsell@vmgl.com

Web: www.franchiseinfo.co.uk

Prysm MFV

Tel: 0117 930 4927

Email: simon@thefranchiseshow.co.uk

Web: www.thefranchiseshow.co.uk

Job Done Marketing

Tel: 0116 242 4157

Email: mark@jobdonemarketing.co.uk

Web: www.jobdonemarketing.co.uk

Franchise Magazines:

Business Franchise Magazine

6th & 7th Floor, 111 Upper Richmond Road, Putney, London, SW15 2TJ

Tel: 020 8394 5216

Email: alison@businessfranchise.com

Franchise World

Highlands House,165 The Broadway, Wimbledon, London, SW19 1NE

Tel: 020 8605 2555

Email: info@franchiseworld.co.uk

The Franchise Magazine

Franchise House, 56 Surrey Street, Norwich, NR1 3FD

Tel: 01603 620301

Email: editorial@fdsltd.com

What Franchise Magazine
Partridge Publications, Third Floor, Gloucester House,
Gloucester Mews, South Street, Eastbourne, East Sussex,
BN21 4XH
Tel: 01323 636004
Email: richard@partridgeltd.co.uk

Making Money
Partridge Publications, Third Floor, Gloucester House,
Gloucester Mews, South Street, Eastbourne, East Sussex,
BN21 4XH
Tel: 01323 636004
Email: richard@partridgeltd.co.uk

Franchise Printed Directories:

FranchiseWorld Directory
Tel: 020 8605 2555
Email: nick@franchiseworld.co.uk
Web: www.franchiseworld.com

The United Kingdom Franchise Directory
Tel: 01603 620301
Email: richardc@fdsltd.com
Web: www.theukfranchisedirectory.net

Newspapers that Cover Franchising:

Daily Express

The Northern & Shell Building, 10 Lower Thames Street, London, EC3R 6EN

Tel: 020 7098 2840

Email: sean.hammond@express.co.uk

Daily Mail

5th Floor, Northcliffe House, 2 Derry Street, London, W8 5TT

Tel: 0161 836 5001

Web: www.mailclassified.co.uk

Daily Mirror

Tel: 020 7293 3434

Email: simon.pitney@mgn.co.uk

Evening Standard

Northcliffe House, 2 Derry Street, London, W8 5EE

Tel: 02073615008

Email: sharon.webber@standatd.co.uk

Sunday Express

The Northern & Shell Building, 10 Lower Thames Street, London, EC3R 6EN

Tel: 020 7098 2840

Email: sean.hammond@express.co.uk

The Mail on Sunday

2 Derry St, London, W8 5TS

Tel: 0207 9387312

Email: joanne.beeney@mailonsunday.co.uk

Franchise Website Directories:

Business Franchise

Tel: 020 8394 5283

Email: Nathalie@businessfranchise.com

Web: www.businessfranchise.com

Franchise Direct

Tel: 03531 865 6370

Email: brian@franchisedirect.co.uk

Web: www.franchisedirect.co.uk

Franchise World

Tel: 020 8605 2555

Email: nick@franchiseworld.co.uk

Web: www.franchiseworld.com

Making Money

Tel: 01323 636000

Email: richard@partridgeltd.co.uk

Web: www.makingmoney.com

Selectyourfranchise

Tel: 023 8027 5710

Email: steve@selectyourfranchise.com

Web: www.selctyourfranchise.com

What Franchise

Tel: 01323 636000

Email: mark@partridgeltd.co.uk

Web: www.whatfranchisemagazine.co.uk

whichfranchise.com

Tel: 0141 204 0050

Email: enquiry@whichfranchise.com

Web: www.whichfranchise.com

AUTHOR PROFILES

CLIVE SAWYER
Managing Director, Business Options

RICHARD HOLDEN
Head of Franchising, Lloyds TSB Commercial

JONATHAN CHADD
Partner, Head of Franchising and IPR Team, Leathes Prior Solicitors

NICOLA BROADHURST
Partner, Head of Franchising, Stevens & Bolton Solicitors

GRAEME PAYNE
Partner, Field Fisher Waterhouse

DERRICK SIMPSON
Managing Director, Franchise Resales Ltd

Author Profile

CLIVE SAWYER
Managing Director, Business Options

Clive is the Managing Director of Business Options, a specialist franchise and business expansion consultancy. Business Options is the *only* Franchise Consultancy accredited by *all* of the following: The British Franchise Association, The Irish Franchise Association, and The Institute of Business Consulting. This ensures that we have the breadth of skills, knowledge and experience to develop the most suitable franchise models for our clients that meets their needs as the franchisor and the future franchisees.

The team at Business Options has over twenty years experience within the Franchising sector. Our experience reflects that we have worked with many different businesses in many different sectors both domestically and internationally. We regularly run franchising seminars for the British Franchise Association seminars and the leading Franchise Banks. Clive Sawyer, Managing Director of Business Options is also a renowned franchising expert and writes articles for the leading franchise magazines as well as being a published author on franchising in the UK.

Clive is also founder, chairman and a director of the Encouraging Women into Franchising Group, which provides advice and guidance to women looking to enter the world of franchising whether as a franchisee or as a business owner looking to franchise their business.

Contact

Tel: 01420 550890

Email: clive.sawyer@businessoptions.biz

Web: www.businessoptions.biz

Author Profile

RICHARD HOLDEN

Head of Franchising, Lloyds TSB Commercial

 Richard joined Lloyds Bank in 1982 and became Head of Franchising in 2004. Prior to this he had many management roles within the Commercial and Retail Banking sectors. He is a strong advocate of ethical franchising and promoting the use of experienced and reputable franchise professionals.

Richard is a regular contributor to the trade and national press on franchising matters and a presenter at seminars and exhibitions about the benefits and pitfalls of franchising as a way to set up in business. Lloyds TSB is one of the most active banks in the franchise sector and his team have a wealth of knowledge to offer the practical support and guidance required by both franchisors and franchisees.

Lloyds TSB, in conjunction with top sector professionals, run several seminars throughout the year for people looking at franchising as a development model for their business. These are must attend events for anyone new to franchising and who wants to learn about how franchising may be suitable for their business. Details of upcoming events are available by contacting the Lloyds TSB Franchise Unit.

Contact

Tel: 0800 681 6078

Email: franchising@lloydstsb.co.uk

Website: www.lloydstsb.com/franchising

Author Profile

JONATHAN CHADD MA (OXON)
Partner, Head of Franchising and IPR Team,
Leathes Prior Solicitors

Leathes Prior is one of East Anglia's leading commercial law firms with a nationally and internationally acknowledged expertise in Franchising and Intellectual Property Law. The team provides a full range of services for franchisors and franchise owners.

The team is headed by Jonathan Chadd, who is recognised by the law directories as one of the UK's leading franchise lawyers with over 30 years experience in advising a wide range of businesses on their expansion both nationally and internationally through franchising and licensing structures. He has particular experience in the retail, business services, healthcare and fast food sectors and provides proactive advice on all aspects of franchising and intellectual property law. His wide international experience includes North America, The Middle East, Australasia, China and India and he is a frequent speaker at national and international franchising events.

Jonathan and his team act for a wide range of different clients from public companies to SMEs (many operating under well known brands) all of whom benefit from the pro-active and highly specialist advice that Leathes Prior can provide together with access to their extensive contacts in the franchise industry.

Contact

Tel: 01603 281102

Email:jchadd@leathesprior.co.uk

www.leathesprior.co.uk

Author Profile

NICOLA BROADHURST
Partner, Head of Franchising, Stevens & Bolton Solicitors

 Nicola is a commercial partner at the eminent South East law firm Stevens & Bolton LLP and heads up its highly experienced franchise team. The franchise team has over 25 years of experience in this sector and offers a full service to franchisors and franchisees including corporate and commercial advice, dispute management, brand protection and employment advice.

Nicola advises on general commercial issues but has a particular specialism in advising on franchise issues, advising both franchisors wishing to franchise existing businesses or expand franchise offerings and franchisees wishing to acquire franchises. Nicola is recommended by a number of franchisors to assist their franchisees in the resale of their franchise businesses. She also advises master franchisees and area developers looking to import franchise systems into the UK and regularly advises clients seeking to franchise internationally. She speaks at numerous specialist franchise seminars and exhibitions and writes for each edition of Franchise World as well as contributing regularly to other franchise publications. She is the firm's designated representative for the British Franchise Association and regularly reviews franchise agreements for accreditation purposes for the BFA. Nicola is ranked in the top tier for the UK for franchise legal advice by Chambers UK 2011.

Contact:

Tel: +44 (0)1483 734228

Email: nicola.broadhurst@stevens-bolton.com

Web: www.stevens-bolton.com

Author Profile

GRAEME PAYNE

Partner, Field Fisher Waterhouse LLP

Graeme is a partner in Field Fisher Waterhouse's Franchising & Intellectual Property Group and specialises in advising clients on how to grow their businesses, brand promotion and the development and commercial exploitation of intellectual property and know how. Graeme's principal sector specialisations are services, leisure, food & beverage, retail and healthcare. He advises individuals and businesses at all stages of development, from individual entrepreneurs and early-stage ventures to multinationals.

Graeme's particular areas of expertise include:
Structuring and drafting UK and international franchise agreements; and advising on, managing and coordinating UK and international franchise roll outs. Graeme co-leads Field Fisher Waterhouse's UK franchise initiatives 'Helping Hand' and 'Incubator' for start up and small to medium sized UK based franchisors. As part of these initiatives Graeme and his team provide the full spectrum of business advice including trade mark and brand protection, structuring, drafting of the franchise documentation and assistance with the roll out. He is a regular speaker at Field Fisher Waterhouse's franchise seminar programme, details of which can be found at Field Fisher Waterhouse's dedicated franchise website www.europeanfranchising.com. Graeme has written articles for *Franchise World*, and has spoken at a number

of national and international franchise seminars and British Franchise Association conferences. Professional memberships include the British Franchise Association, the International Bar Association, the American Bar Association and the International Franchise Association.

Contact:

Tel: +44 (0)20 7861 4685:

Email: graeme.payne@ffw.com

Web: www.europeanfranchising.com

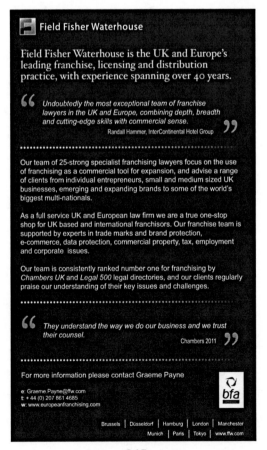

Author Profile

DERRICK SIMPSON

Managing Director, Franchise Resales LTD

 Derrick has played an active role within franchising since 1988 mainly in Kall Kwik moving into the area for which he is best known – reselling existing franchises. After a short time in the Myhome Group he established Franchise Resales. Refining and extending his system to become the highly structured and effective Franchise Resales process. An active supporter of the BFA Derrick is a member of the BFA Board. He is a BFA accredited Qualified Franchise Professional and a member of the QFP assessment panel. A regular speaker at BFA events on matters around franchise resales and often consulted by existing members for advice on the subject.

The Franchise Resales team manage resales using their proven system and Toolkit to support both seller and purchaser throughout the process. Managing the entire 'end to end' process from prospectus writing, sourcing prospects, franchisor approval, negotiations, funding and coordinating the legal process in line with the franchisor's requirements. Franchise Resales also deliver Exit Planning Seminars at franchisors meetings and conferences as required. Franchise Resales additionally advise franchisors on their own exit route and manage the resale of entire franchise networks and master licences. They provide the UK franchise community and prospective purchasers with a total resales solution.

Contact:

Tel: 01562 881 023

Email: derricks@franchiseresales.co.uk

Web: www.franchiseresales.co.uk

If you found this book useful, you will also be interested in Clive's first book...

HOW TO FRANCHISE YOUR BUSINESS

The plain speaking guide for business owners

CLIVE SAWYER

How To Franchise Your Business

The plain speaking guide
for business owners

by Clive Sawyer

*Available from Amazon and
www.liveitpublishing.com*

"Essential reading for business owners
considering franchising their business."

Richard Holden, Head of Franchising, Lloyds Banking Group

Clive Sawyer, Managing Director of Business Options, one of the UK's leading Franchise and Business Expansion Consultancies, has written this book to cut through the confusion and complexity surrounding franchising a business.

Clive, in his renowned plain speaking manner helps the reader assess whether franchising is the right expansion model for them. He then leads the reader, step by step through everything they will need to know.

For anyone serious about franchising their business, this book is essential reading.

lip

ATTENTION WRITERS

Do you want to get published?

Live It Publishing is seeking new and exciting Authors
in the fields of self-help, business, health, mind body & spirit
and personal development.

We want to help you turn your creative work into a reality and
give your professional credibility a massive boost!

To discover more about getting your book published and
distributed across a global network visit us at:

www.liveitpublishing.com

LIP... The easiest way to get published!

Lightning Source UK Ltd.
Milton Keynes UK
UKOW031136300613

213011UK00002B/48/P